PYTHON FOR BEGINNERS:

AN ESSENTIAL GUIDE TO LEARN WITH BASIC EXERCISES: PYTHON PROGRAMMING CRASH COURSE FOR DATA ANALYSIS AND FOR BEGINNER HAKERS

Table of Contents

Description 1

Introduction 5

Chapter 1: Why python... 7

Chapter 2: Python for Data Analysis – Basics 13

Python REPL.. 13

Python Basic - Data Types and Operators 14

Basic Containers – Lists and Tuples 21

Modules.. 24

Conditional Statements.. 26

Loops 27

Extra – Zen of Python 29

Exercises.. 30

Chapter 3: Python Operators 37

Arithmetic Operators 37

Assignment Operators.. 38

Membership Operators 40

Identity Operators 42

Chapter 4: Supervised Learning Algorithms 45

Regression... 45

K-Nearest Neighbors.. 46

Chapter 5: Creating & Accessing Your Python Dictionary . 51

Creating and Combining Strings 53

Accessing and Updating Strings................................... 58

Chapter 6: Introducing Variables..........................**63**

Integers, Strings and Floats Oh My!.............................. 65

Performing Operations on Variables............................. 67

Chapter 7: Naming Conventions and Comments **71**

Using Comments.. 72

Chapter 8: Handling Inputs **73**

Chapter 9: Working with the Conditional Statements **79**

Chapter 10: Exception Handling in the Python Language..**87**

Chapter 11: Functions, Classes and Methods **95**

Introduction to OOP 95

Chapter 12: Using Linear Regression for Predictions **105**

Simple Linear Regression.................................... 105

Chapter 13: Replacing and Correcting words **115**

Chapter 14: Using Jupyter notebook for user interaction **127**

Display tabular data in IPython notebook 127

Adding user interaction.................................... 129

Chapter 15: The Regular Expressions............................ **141**

Chapter 16: Data Visualization with Python **149**

Conclusion.. **165**

Description

When it comes to picking out the coding language that you want to work with, there are a lot of different options that you can go with. Some are going to provide you with a lot of power. Some are going to work specifically with certain operating systems. And others are going to work the best when it comes to working on a website or online. But one of the best coding languages for you to work with that will help improve your coding experience and will help you to do a lot of different programming applications, then you have to learn how to work with Python.

Python is going to be a great coding language that helps you to really do a good job with many applications online and for programs that you want to make. It is easy enough for a beginner to use, in fact, it was designed to be used by those who are beginners and who have never coded before, while still having the strength that you need to handle some of the different harder applications, such as machine learning, that you would like to explore.

There are a lot of different benefits that come with using the Python language and this is why so many people like to spend time learning how to work with this kind of language. There are some benefits that you are going to enjoy when you decide to learn how to code with Python.

There are a lot of different support libraries that you are able to use. You will be able to find an extension and a library that works with Python for almost anything that you need. These libraries are great for providing you with the algorithms, the functions, and more that you need in order to get any coding task that you want to be done. You can work with just the traditional library that comes with Python originally, or you can go through and work with some of the other extensions and libraries based on the kind of project you would like to do.

Another benefit that comes with this coding language is all of the different integration features that happen. Python can be a good thing to a programmer because it is going to integrate what is known as the Enterprise Application Integration. This is going to be useful because it can make sure that you can work with different operating systems, different coding languages, and more. There is almost nothing that Python isn't able to help you out with, so learning how to use it can be so great.

Python is also going to provide you with more productivity in the process. The language here is going to be designed as an object-oriented language, and it includes many different kinds of support libraries to help you get things done. Because of these resources, and the ease of use that comes with this language, the programmer is going to be able to get more done in a shorter amount of time. This can even help to improve how much productivity the programmer is going to enjoy while using some different coding languages along with Python.

This guide will focus on the following:

- Why python
- Python for Data Analysis – Basics
- Python Operators
- Supervised Learning Algorithms
- Creating & Accessing Your Python Dictionary
- Introducing Variables
- Naming Conventions and Comments
- Handling Inputs
- Working with the Conditional Statements
- Exception Handling in the Python Language
- Functions, Classes and Methods
- Using Linear Regression for Predictions
- Replacing and Correcting words
- Using Jupyter notebook for user interaction
- The Regular Expressions
- Data Visualization with Python... AND MORE!!!

Introduction

Running Python on a computer has proven to be a success. As a beginner in Python, it is key to keep your mind wide open for new encounters. The above, are the steps required to ensure that your computer is running python smoothly.

Remain focused, as you are on this journey to learning programming. You will not become great overnight. It is always a great thing to see a programmer turn into a millionaire or a programmer changing the lives of thousands in a single programming day.

Ultimately this book was written with the goal in mind of teaching you not necessarily about Python, but programming at large.

If you are reading this, it means that you have made it to the end of the book. One word for you?

When you make a clear and realistic plan of how you aim to learn, the plan becomes achievable. Learning will definitely be at your own pace. The first step is the interest that you had, which resulted in you reading this book and then – action! Challenge yourself with new tasks every day. Programming is not as hard as it looks or as hard as people make it seem. Nothing is hard if you are ready to put in the work. Start with the basics.

Most of the people who are new to programming and who want to learn use Python. Even though most programmers say it is an easy program to learn, it will all depend on you. If you are to have a chance at being successful in this, you will need to go the extra mile. Ask questions from experts and always be ready and eager to learn. Who knows? This could be a step-in learning all the programming languages out there. Keep an open mind and you will not find anything hard about this.

Do something with it. You can absolutely use this book as a reference, but it wasn't written to necessarily be one - this book was written in order to teach you the essence of programming and everything that you need to do to start programming in Python, as well as the essential tools of the language that you'll have to know how to use as a beginner.

Chapter 1: Why python

One of the difficulties that developers face when working with joint processing in the Python programming language (in particular, CPython, the reference implementation of Python written in C) is GIL. The GIL mechanism is a deadlock mechanism that protects access to Python objects, preventing the simultaneous execution of Python byte codes in multiple threads. This locking is necessary mainly because CPython's memory management is not thread-safe. CPython uses a reference counter to implement its memory management. This results in the fact that multiple threads can access and execute Python code at the same time; this situation is undesirable and it can cause incorrect data processing and we say that this type of memory management is not oriented towards multi-threaded management. To solve this problem, there is a GIL, as its name indicates, a certain lock that allows only one thread to access the code and Python objects. However, this also means that in order to implement programs with multiple threads in CPython, developers must be aware of the GIL and circumvent it. It is for this reason that many who have problems implementing co-processing systems in Python.

So why do we even use Python for collaborative processing? Even though GIL does not allow CPython programs with multiple threads to get all the advantages of multiprocessor systems in certain situations, most of the operations with blocking or long-term execution, such as input / output, image processing, as well as grinding numbers in NumPy, occur outside the existing one. Gil Thus, the GIL itself becomes a potential bottleneck only for programs with many threads that spend significant time inside the GIL. For example, applications with many processes that do not share any common resources between processes, such as input / output, image processing, or grinding NumPy numbers, can work seamlessly with GIL.

In addition, Python has gained increasing popularity in the programming community. Thanks to user-friendly syntax and general readability, more and more people believe that it is relatively easy to use Python in their development, whether it's a beginner learning a new programming language, users with an average level of training in searching for available modern Python functionality, or experienced Programmers using Python to solve complex problems. There are estimates that Python code development can be up to 10 times faster than C / C ++ coding.

A large number of developers using Python have come about as a result of a powerful, still growing community. Every day, Python libraries and packages are developed and released, supplying various tasks and technologies. Currently, Python supports an incredibly wide range of programming - namely, software development, GUI workstations, video game design, web and Internet development, as well as scientific and numerical calculations. In recent years, Python has also grown as one of the top tools in data science, Big Data, and machine learning, competing with a long-term player in the field, R.

The huge number of development tools available in Python has prompted an increasing number of developers to start programming in Python, which makes Python even more popular and easy to use; I call it the vicious circle of Python . David Robinson, DataCamp's research supervisor, wrote a blog post about Python's incredible growth and called it the most popular programming language.

However, Python is slow, at least slower than other popular programming languages. This is because Python is a dynamic typing language that interprets in which values are not stored in tight buffers, but in scattered objects. This is a direct result of the readability and usability of Python. Fortunately, there are various options for making your Python program run faster, with concurrency being one of the most difficult among them; and this is exactly what we are going to master in this book.

Customizing Your Python Environment

Before we move on, let's go through a number of descriptions about how to configure the necessary tools that you will use in this book.

General installation

Let's look at the actual process of obtaining a certain Python distribution for your system and the corresponding development environment:

All developers can get their own Pyton distribution from https: / / www.python. Org / downloads / .

Even though both versions of Python 2 and Python 3 are supported and maintained, throughout this book we will use Python 3.

For this book, a flexible option would be an IDE (integrated development environment). Although it is technically possible to develop Python applications with a minimal text editor such as Notepad or TextEdit, it is usually much easier to read and write code using an IDE purposefully developed for Python. They include: IDLE , PyCharm , Sublime Text, and Atom .

Sample Code Unloading

To get the code that has been used throughout this book, you can download the repository from GitHub, which contains all the examples and project code described in the book:

To get started, visit https: / / github.com/ PacktPublishing / Mastering- Concurrency-in-Python .

To upload the corresponding repository, simply click on the Clone or download button in the upper right corner of your window. Select Download ZIP to download the necessary compressed repository to your computer:

To download the necessary repository, click on Download ZIP

Unzip the downloaded file to create the folder we are looking for. This folder should have a name Mastering-Concurrency-in-Python.

findings

Now you have learned the basics of the concepts of joint and parallel programming. All this relates to the design and structural programming of commands and instructions so that different sections of your program can be executed in some kind of effective way, and at the same time share the same resources. Since when some commands and instructions are executed at the same time, time is saved, parallel programming provides a significant improvement in the execution time of the program when compared with traditional sequential programming.

However, when designing a parallel program, various factors should be taken into account. While there are special tasks that can easily be divided into independent sections that can be executed in parallel (stunning parallel tasks), others require different types of coordination between the existing program commands so that such shared resources can be applied correctly and efficiently. There are also tasks with sequential processing that is intrinsically intrinsic to them, in which no joint processing and parallelism can be applied to obtain program acceleration. You should be aware of such fundamental differences between these tasks so that you can carefully design your co-processing programs.

In recent times, a paradigm shift has occurred that facilitated the implementation of joint processing in most aspects of the existing programming universe. Now joint processing can be found everywhere: desktop and mobile applications, video games, web and Internet development, AI and so on. Collaborative processing is still growing and is expected to continue to grow in the future. Therefore, it is extremely important for any experienced programmer to understand the joint processing and related concepts, as well as to know how to integrate these concepts into their applications.

Python, on the other hand, is one of the most (if not the most) popular programming languages. It provides options in most programming sub-sectors. Combining collaborative processing and Python in this way is one of the most important topics to learn and master in programming.

Chapter 2: Python for Data Analysis – Basics

Now that we have everything setup, we can start to get used to the programming language. Therefore, we will go in details about the basic syntax, flow control blocks and intrinsic peculiarities. All these topics work as a presentation to the language for new users, or as a reminder for readers with a good knowledge.

Python REPL

As soon as the Python installation is completed, we can immediately start to use it interactively using its Read Eval Print Loop (REPL). It works as a dynamics script in which you can create and modify variables and see instant results.

The main advantage of the REPL is that you can start experimenting right away. Therefore, it works as a great tool to test basic syntax of the language. If any code is taking too long to run in the REPL

§ Starting the REPL

To run it, you just need to or search for "Python" or type python in the command line:

§ Interface

At first glance, it seems like just another CLI. Initially, it shows basic information of the installed Python version.

§ Input Field

The input field is represented by the triple '>' symbol, it is where the commands/script should be typed.

Python Basic - Data Types and Operators

Now, let's be familiar with all the basics types and operations of the language.

Comments

Any command starting with "#" are completely ignored.

Basic Data Types

As many programming languages, Python has all the standard data types implemented.

If you want to know a type of any object in Python, just use *type(object)* and the resulting type will be shown (which is a class in Python).

§ Numeric and Boolean Data Types

Type	Description	Examples
int	Integer type	354, 56, -42
float	Floating point type can be represented in scientific notation. 1e3 = 1x103=1000.	8.5, 0.0, - 1.7e-5
bool	Boolean value	True, False

§ Strings

In Python Strings are expressed in double ("...") or singles ('...') quotes. If you want to quote in your string, you can scape them using \, or use a different quote in its definition.

Strings in python are represented by the class str. Different of some programming languages, Python doesn't have a character type. Therefore, a single character is also a string. Additionally, strings have many built-in methods that facilitate its manipulation and transformation. Most of these methods will be presented later in the book. Also, should be noted that strings are immutable objects, therefore their values can not be altered. If you want a different string, a new one should be created. You can cast different types to strings using the *str()* function.

§ None Type

The *None* keyword represents the *NoneType* in Python. It is a type that represents no values. In general, it is used to show that a function did not resulted in any values.

Variable Assignment

Assignment represents the binding of a name to a value or expression. As in multiple programming languages, variable assignment is done using the (=) operator. Variable names are case sensitive, and keyword of the language cannot be used to represent variables names. You can have simple, multiple and same values assignments.

Arithmetic Operators

Most arithmetic operators work just like expected between numeric values.

Operator	Description	Examples
+	Adds the 2 values	>>> 3 + 5 8
-	Subtracts the values	>>> 8 - 4 4

*	Multiply values	>>> 21 * 2 42
/	Divide the values, the returned values are always a float.	>>> 15 / 2 7.5
//	Floor division, it ignores any fractional values from results	>>> 15 / 2 7
%	Modulus, returns the remainder of the division	>>> 6 % 4 2
**	Raises to power	>>> 2**8 256
()	Ranks the order of operations	>>> (1 + 3) / 2 2.0

OBS1.: Operations between bool and int/float are automatically converted to the numeric type (int/float). In which True is 1 and False is 0.

OBS2.: Operations between float and int are automatically converted to float type.

OBS3.: The operators + and * have a special effect on str type. For example:

As can be seen from the examples above, the str*int operation repeats the string values multiple times, and the str+str concatenates the strings.

§ Precedence and Associativity

Each operator has a precedence in that expression. In other words, some operations are solved before other. The order is shown in the table below:

Order	Operators	Description
1	( )	Parentheses
2	**	Exponent
3	-x, +x	Unary minus or plus
4	*, /, //, %	Multiplication, division, floor division, modulus
5	+, -	Addition, subtraction

Operators with same precedence are solved by their associativity order.

Associativity	Operators	Example
Left-to-right	( ), **, *, /, //, %, +, -	>>> 5/2%2 0.5
Right-to-left	**	>>> 2**2**3 256

This means that any expression will follow this order for resolution. First, the order in *Precedence Table*, then the order in *Associativity Table*.

§ Self-Increment

Multiple times, it is necessary to increment a variable. There is a small shortcut to perform this using the operators seen before. The shortcut operations and their representation are shown below.

Operator	Example	Equivalent Representation
+=	x += 2	x = x + 2
-=	x -= 3	x = x − 3
*=	x *= 4	x = x * 4

| /= | x /= 5 | x = x / 5 |
| %/ | x %= 6 | x = x % 6 |

2.2.5. Comparison Operators

Values or expressions can be compared in Python using the comparison operators, the result of this assessment is a bool type.

Operator	Meaning	Examples
>, <	Greater/lesser than	>>> 3 > 2 True
>=, <=	Greater/less than or equal	>>> 4 <= 2 + 2 True
= =	Equal to	>>> 6 == 2 * 3 True
!=	Different of	>>> 3 != 3 False

OBS.: You can compare multiple things in Python but be careful with the result of the comparison. For example, strings can be compared, but results in the comparison between their ASCII values of their characters. Therefore, careful when using these operators with non-numeric types.

§ Boolean Logic

When you want to combine multiple Boolean logic operations you can use and, or, not keywords. When used with Boolean values, operator and returns true only when both are true, operator or returns true when at least one is true, not inverts the Boolean value.

Basic Containers – Lists and Tuples

There are two basic types of ordered sequences in Python: list and tuple. Both stores ordered values but have a crucial difference: mutability. While list can be easily modified, tuples (just like strings) are immutable. Due to this difference, they are used in different cases. In general, lists are used when you need to modify, remove or append values, while tuples when you only need to read the values. Thanks to the immutable restriction, iterations on tuples are faster than on lists.

Lists

They can contain multiple types of data. To define a list, you just need to write a sequence of comma-separated values between square brackets.

§ Defining Lists

Square brackets are used in list definitions.

§ Function list()

Beyond creating an empty list, you can also create list from previous objects such as strings.

§ Indexing

Each value of the list is accessible by an index. The index represents position of the value in the list, starting by position 0. Additionally, negative index can be used counting from the end of the list. As lists are mutable, the index can also be used to change the values.

§ Slicing

Sometimes, instead of accessing a single value from a list, you could want to select a sub-list. For this, there is the slicing operation. Generally, slicing is used with [start:end] resulting in values from the start position until the end, the end position is excluded of the resulting substring. If omitted, the start defaults to 0 and the end to the length of the list. Furthermore, slicing can be used to change multiple values at once. The examples below show how slicing works.

A good way to create intuition about how slicing works is to think of the indexes as points between the values.

In the image above, slicing [-4:-1] returns [12, 13, 14] and [0:2] return [11, 12].

§ Concatenating and Repeating

Like strings, the operators + and * can be used to concatenate and repeat lists, respectively. The result is a new list. Additionally, *list*'s have the method *append* that attaches a value to its end.

Tuples

Tuples are immutable and can contain multiple types of data. Therefore, they are generally used to read static data.

§ Defining Tuples

Parenthesis are used to define tuples. To differentiate a tuple with a single value to a simple parenthesis expression it must contain a comma. Examples:

§ Function tuple()

Like lists, you can also create tuples from previous objects such as strings or lists.

§ Indexing

Just like lists, tuples can be indexed, and the same indexing rules are applied except for modifying its values. Examples:

§ Slicing

Tuples support slicing too. Of course, not allowing change of the values.

§ Concatenating and Repeating

The operators + and * works like lists. As tuples are not mutable the result is a new tuple created from the concatenation or repetition. Examples:

Function len

The *len* function can be used in most containers types. It shows the number of elements in this container whether a *list, tuple* or *string*. Some examples that show its usage.

Modules

The *Python REPL* is great to test small code snippets and language syntax. However, after closed, all the variables and operations defined are lost. Therefore, to write longer programs and save the results a text editor is necessary. In the editor, you can create a new file that contains the instructions and variable definitions, this file is called a script. Python scripts are saved with the *.py* extension.

§ Running Scripts

Consider a script called *myscript.py*. In order to run this script, follow these instructions:

1.

Open your system terminal.

2.

Navigate to the script folder (where the *myscript.py* file is located).

3.

Run the command:

After all code in the script will be executed in the current terminal window.

Try to run the examples below. Paste their code in the text editor and save a example1.py and example2.py files. Then follow the instructions above to see the code outputs.

```
Example 1 - example1.py
# This is a comment

a = 5

print(a)
OUTPUT
5
```

```
Example 2 - example2.py
# This is a comment

b = 21 * 2

print(b)
OUTPUT
42
```

After invoking the modules, their instructions will be executed.

OBS.: In Visual Studio Code, the script could be executed directly in the IDE using the run button.

Conditional Statements

Like other languages, the code under the *if* statement is only executed if the expression is evaluated as *True*. Additionally, the optional *else* keyword can be used to execute another code when the statement is *False*. The overall format is show below.

The example shows the overall syntax of the *if* and *else* statements. Here we can see an important aspect of the Python programming language: *Indentation*.

§ Indentation

Indentation describes the spaces between the left margin and the start of text. In Python, indentation mean that the code belongs to a *block of code*, in other words, it indicates whether a line is in the same block or not. Commonly, 2 or 4 "white spaces" or 1 "tab" can be used for indentation. However, it is highly recommended to only one kind should be used throughout the code, either whitespaces of tabs.

§ Multiple Conditions

Sometimes we need to test various conditions, for this we can have multiple *if...else* statements. Additionally, a shorter term for *else if* statements can be used: *elif*.

Here we used the *print* function to show the results.

§ Nested Statements

In order to test multiple dependent conditions, if statements can be nested together, resulting in various blocks of code.

Loops

There are two basic loops in Python, *for* and *while*. Both are used to loop through a block of code but have different use-cases.

While

The *while* loop repeats a block of code while a given expression is evaluated as True. The condition is tested before each execution.

Since evaluation occurs before the block execution the block might not even run. Notice the presence of *indentation* for the block of code.

In the examples above we can see how while loop works. After each code block execution, the expression is re-evaluated to check if the block will be re-run again.

For

When you need a finer control for the total number of executions, the *for* loop is used. In python, *for loop* uses a sequence of elements defined as an *iterator*. The for loop iterates over each value in this sequence.

During each pass through the loop, a new value from the sequence is passed to the variable *VALUE*, until the sequence end is reached. Pay attention to the use of the *in* keyword before the operator.

OBS1.: As in any other programming language, it is highly discouraged to modify the iterating object during the loop, since this can easily cause undesired behaviour.

OBS2.: The in keyword are also used to see if a value is present in a sequence (list, tuple, string, ...). In this case it returns a Boolean value.

§ Iterators

Simply put, an *iterator* corresponds a sequence of elements. In Python, *lists*, *tuples* and *strings* are example of iterable objects. If you want to create a sequence of integer to iterate over, the *range* function can be used.

The examples bellow shows different kinds of iterators being used in for loops.

§ Range Function

This built-in function created a sequence of integers. It can be used with 1, 2 or 3 arguments. With one argument, the sequence starts from 0 until the given argument (excluded) with step unitary. Using with two arguments, the first correspond to initial(included) value or the sequence and the second to the final (excluded) value. Finally, with three arguments is like with two, but the third argument corresponds to the increment size. Check the examples below.

The examples show the usage of the range function and in the for loop. By now, you could have noticed that the *range* function could be used to generate index for elements in lists. Indeed, this could be done, but using the sequence directly would be a more "Pythonic" approach. The example below illustrates this case.

As you can see, the range function can be used to generate index of each element in a list but looping using the sequence directly is a more simple and understandable code.

Extra – Zen of Python

As a small Easter egg, Python has a collection of guiding principles for writing computer programs. You can check this by running the command bellow in the Python REPL.

After running the command, a text from Tim Peters will be printed. It shows the principles that were considered in the design of Python as a programming language.

Even though this is an Easter egg, all these tips are valuable, and any programmer should keep them in mind when creating new projects.

Exercises

Answer the question below, then and check your responses using the *Python REPL*.

What's the type of each of these expressions?

```
>>> 1e-3
```

```
>>> 2
```

```
>>> 3.
```

```
>>> 5 > 2
```

The string definition below are valid? Mark as True of False.

```
>>> "String\'s"                    (  )
>>> "HelloWorld'                    (  )
>>> 'This is a "quote"'             (  )
>>> 'That's fine!'                  (  )
```

What are the results of the operations?

```
>>> -3 * 1
```

```
>>> 5 % 3
```

```
>>> 2 + 3 * 3
```

```
>>> 1e1 + 1.5
```

```
>>> True + 3
```

```
>>> 3 ** False
```

```
>>> type(3 / 3)
```

```
>>> type(3. + 2)
```

```
>>> type(False + True)
```

```
>>> '123' * 2
```

```
>>> 'Hello' + "World"
```

```
>>> 2 - 2 / 4
```

>>> (2 - 2) / 4

>>> -1e1 + 8 // (1. + 1)

>>> 2 ** 2 ** 4

>>> 3 ** False

>>> 3 % 5 + (2 ** (6 / 3))

What are the results of the sequence of commands?

>>> a = b = 3

>>> c, d = 1, 2

>>> a + c == d * b - 2

>>> s = "a"

>>> s *= 3

>>> s + "b"

>>> a = 0

>>> a != 0 and True

```
>>> b = c = 42

>>> b /= 2

>>> b != 21 or c/b == 2
>>> b = False

>>> c = not b

>>> ((not c) and b) or True
>>> a = [1]

>>> a * 11
>>> a = [1, 2]

>>> b = [3, 4]

>>> a + b
```

Consider the list li = [42, 1, 2, 3, 'A', 'B'], what the result of each alternative?

a) >>> li[3]

b) >>> li[-2]

c) >>> li[:-3]

d) >>> li[-5:]

Which of the alternatives throws an error when executed?

>>> a = (1,2,3)

>>> a[3]
>>> b = [5, 6, 7, 8]

>>> b[-5]
>>> a = (1, 2)

>>> b = (3, 4)

>>> c = a / b
>>> a = (1,2,3)

>>> b = (1,2,3)

>>> a + b
>>> a = (1,2,3)

>>> b = (1,2,3)

```
>>> a * b
```

Write a script to solve the problem: consider a list of size n, if n is odd the script shows the value in the middle of the list, if n is even, it shows the two values at the center of the list.

Examples:

list1 = [1,5,11,12,16] -> 11

list2 = [1,5,11,12] -> [5, 11]

Chapter 3: Python Operators

Python operators help us manipulate the value of operands in operations. Example:

10 * 34 = 340

In the above example, the values 10 and 34 are known as operands, while * is known as the operator. Python supports different types of operators.

Arithmetic Operators

These are the operators used for performing basic mathematical operations. They include multiplication (*), addition (+), subtraction (-), division (/), modulus (%) and others. Example:

#!/usr/bin/python3

n1 = 6

n2 = 5

n3 = 0

n3 = n1 + n2

print("The value of sum is: ", n3)

n3 = n1 - n2

print("The result of subtraction is: ", n3)

n3 = n1 * n2

```
print("The result of multiplication is:", n3)

n3 = n1 / n2

print ("The result of division is: ", n3 )

n3 = n1 % n2

print ("The remainder after division is: ", n3)

n1 = 2

n2 = 3

n3 = n1**n2

print ("The exponential value is: ", n3)

n1 = 20

n2 = 4

n3 = n1//n2

print ("The result of floor division is: ", n3)
```

The code prints the followig when executed:

Assignment Operators

These operators the combination of the assignment operator (=) with the other operators. A good example of an assignment operator is "+=". The expression p+=q means "p=p + q". The expression "p/=q" means that "p=p / q". The assignment operators involve combining the assignment operator with the rest of the other operators.

Example:

#!/usr/bin/python3

n1 = 6

n2 = 5

n3 = 0

n3 = n1 + n2

print ("The value of n3 is: ", *n3)*

n3 += n1

print ("The value of n3 is: ", *n3)*

n3 *= n1

print ("The value of n3 is: ", *n3)*

n3 /= n1

print ("The value of n3 ", *n3)*

n3 = 2

n3 %= n1

print ("The value of n3 is: ", *n3)*

n3 **= n1

print ("The value of n3 is: ", *n3)*

n3 //= n1

print ("The value of n3 is: ", *n3)*

The code will print the following when executed:

The statement "n3 = n1 + n2" is very straight forward as we are just adding the value of n1 to that of n2. In the expression "n3 += n1", we are adding the value of n3 to that of n1 and then assign the result to n3. However, note that in the previous statement, the value of n3 changed to "11" after adding n1 to n2. So we have 11+6, which gives 17. After that, the new value of the variable n3 will be 17. The expression "n3 *= n1" means "n3= n3 * n1". This will be 17 * 6, and the result will be 102. That is how these operators work in Python!

Membership Operators

These are the operators which are used for testing membership in a certain sequence of elements. The sequence of elements can be a string, a list or a tuple. The two membership operators include "in" and "not in".

The "in" operator returns true if the value you specify is found in the sequence. The operator "not in" will evaluate to a true if the specified element is not found in the sequence.

Example:

#!/usr/bin/python3

n1 = 7

n2 = 21

ls = [10, 20, 30, 40, 50]

if (n1 in ls):

```
    print ("n1 was found in the list")

else:

    print ("n1 was not found in the list")

if ( n2 not in ls ):

    print ("n2 was not found in the list")

else:

    print ("n2 was found in the list")

n3=n2/n1
if ( n3 in ls ):

    print ("n1 was found in the list")

else:

    print ("n1 was not found in the list")
```

The code will print the following once executed:

The value of num1 is 7. This is not part of our list, and that is why the use of the "in" operator returns a false. This causes the "else" part to be executed. The value of n2 is 21. This is not on the list. This expression returns a true, and the first part below the expression is executed. 21 divide by 7 is 3. This value is not on the list. The use of the last "in" operator evaluates to a false, and that is why the "else" part below it is executed.

Identity Operators

These operators are used to compare the values of two memory locations. Python has a method named "id()" that returns the unique identifier of the object. Python has two identity operators:

- is- this operator evaluates to a true in case the variables used on either side of the operator are pointing to a similar object. It evaluates to false otherwise.
- is not- this operator evaluates to a false if the variables on either side of the operator are pointing to a similar object, and true otherwise.

Example:

#!/usr/bin/python3

n1 = 45

n2 = 45

print ('The initial values are','n1=',*n1*,':',*id(n1)*, 'n2=',*n2*,':',*id(n2)*)

if (n1 is n2):

   print ("1. n1 and n2 share an identity")

else:

   print ("2. n1 and n2 do not share identity")

if (id(n1) == id(n2)):

   print ("3. n1 and n2 share an identity")

else:

   print *("4. n1 and n2 do not share identity")*

n2 = 100

print *('The variable values are','n1=',n1,':',id(n1),*
'n2=',n2,':',id(n2))

if *(n1 is not n2):*

   print *("5. n1 and n2 do not share identity")*

else:

   print *("6. n1 and n2 share identity")*

The code will print the following once executed:

Note that I have numbered some of the print statements so that it may be easy to differentiate them. In the first instance, the values of variables n1 and n2 are equal. The first statement of the output shows the respective values for the variables together with their unique identifier. Note that the identifier has been obtained by use if the id() Python method and the name of the variable has been passed inside the function as the argument. The expression "if (n1 is n2):" will evaluate to a true since the values of the two variables are equal, or they are pointing to a similar object. This is why the print statement labeled 1 was executed!

You must also have noticed that the unique identifiers of the two variables are equal. In the expression "if (id(n1) == id(n2)):", we are testing whether the values of the identifiers for the two variables are the same. This evaluates to a true, hence the print statement labeled 3 has been executed!

The expression "n2 = 100" changes the value of variable n2 from 45 to 100. At this point, the values of the two variables will not be equal. This is because n1 has a value of 45, while n2 has a value of 100. This is clearly in the next print statement which shows the values of the variables together with their corresponding ids. You must also have noticed that the ids of the two variables are not equal at this point.

The expression "if (n1 is not n2):" evaluates to a true, hence the print statement labeled 5 was executed. If we test to check whether the values of the ids for the two variables are equal, you will notice that they are not equal.

Chapter 4: Supervised Learning Algorithms

So far you only had a brief encounter with supervised learning; however, now you are equipped with enough knowledge to start working with this type of algorithm. Just take note that, in the real world, you will rarely apply only one type of algorithm. You will often have to combine different supervised learning techniques as well as unsupervised ones.

In this chapter, you will learn about the most important supervised machine learning algorithms, such as regression and K-nearest neighbors and how they are used. You will continue working with a variety of datasets that you need to download before putting everything into practice.

Regression

Most machine learning projects will involve regression as one of the problem-solving techniques. You will have two options, namely logistic regression and linear regression. Both types of algorithms offer highly accurate results, but they each fulfil their own purpose.

The goal of linear regression is to process the independent variables in order to predict a value. This makes it the ideal algorithm when you need to establish a relationship between multiple variables.

Logistic regression, however, doesn't truly live up to its name because its purpose is to deal with classification. However, for now, we will focus on linear regression.

K-Nearest Neighbors

This is one of the most basic supervised machine learning algorithms you can apply to solve both regression and classification problems. While it is simple in design, it can also be used in extremely complex applications. In fact, its simplicity is one of the main reasons it's so efficient.

The technique involves working with labeled data. Let's say we have two different training observations and you need to discover the connection between them. If we already know the input of the first one, we can apply the algorithm to figure out the value of the second. The algorithms determine the distance between one data point and another, making the calculations between all the existing points. Once it is calculated, a K point will be defined and it will be an integer data type. A class is then created, and it will contain the data point which will be neighboring the location with the vast majority of all K points.

Keep in mind that this type of algorithm is best suited when dealing with complex data. To illustrate its use, we are going to use Scikit-learn once again in order to extract an open-source dataset. We will be using the MNIST digits dataset, which contains 60,000 pictures that are meant to be used as training data and another 10,000 for testing. Keep in mind that Scikit isn't a must have because you can find this dataset on multiple websites as it is open for all. However, this tool just makes everything much easier. Furthermore, we will not be using the entire dataset. It is too large for a simple demonstration meant to illustrate the practical use of this algorithm. Therefore, we will only extract 1,000 samples. Don't forget that the higher the number of samples, the more it will take for your system to process and analyze everything. Now, let's import what we need:

In: from sklearn.utils import shuffle

from sklearn.datasets import

from sklearn.cross_validation import train_test_split

import pickle

mnist = pickle.load(open("mnist.pickle", "rb"))

mnist.data, mnist.target = shuffle(mnist.data, mnist.target)

These are our preparatory steps. We have imported Scikit-learn, as well as the dataset we need. In addition, we have used the pickle module which handles something known as "pickling". This feature will introduce you to Python object serializations. What this means is that you can take an object and convert it into a data type that we can store. Furthermore, object serialization also allows you to go in reverse by reverting the stored data to its previous state. The purpose of this feature is to allow you to communicate data structures through a network.

The next step is to reduce the dataset to the number of samples we want. Right now, we have the entire set imported. Type the following lines:

```
mnist.data = mnist.data[:1000]

mnist.target = mnist.target[:1000]

X_train, X_test, y_train, y_test = train_test_split(mnist.data,

mnist.target, test_size=0.8, random_state=0)

In: from sklearn.neighbors import KNeighborsClassifier

# KNN: K=10, default measure of Euclidean distance

clf = KNeighborsClassifier(3)

clf.fit(X_train, y_train)

y_pred = clf.predict(X_test)
```

In this block of code, we simply applied the theory explained above. Take note that, as a metric for the K distance, we use a Euclidean distance. There are other types we can use, but as a beginner, you shouldn't worry about them right now. The next step is to check how the algorithm performed. This is done with the help of a classification report that you call for by typing:

```
In: from sklearn.metrics import classification_report

print (classification_report(y_test, y_pred))
```

There results should look something like this:

Out:

precision	recall	f1-score	support	
0.00.68	0.90	0.78		79
1.0	0.66	1.00	0.79	95
2.0	0.83	0.50	0.62	76
3.0	0.59	0.64	0.61	85
4.0	0.65	0.56	0.60	75
5.0	0.76	0.55	0.64	80
6.0	0.89	0.69	0.77	70
7.0	0.76	0.83	0.79	76
8.0	0.91	0.56	0.69	77
9.0	0.61	0.75	0.67	87
avg / total	0.73	0.70	0.70	800

We don't have the best possible performance, but good enough for the purpose of this exercise. Keep in mind that in order to achieve an accuracy of above 0.9 you would have to pre-process your data better and use additional algorithms to further improve the result. With that being said, let's glance at the training speed, but let's also take a look at the training speed with the following lines:

In: %timeit clf.fit(X_train, y_train)

Out: 1000 loops, best of 3: 1.67 ms per loop

In: %timeit clf.predict(X_test)

Out: 10 loops, best of 3: 181 ms per loop

You'll notice that this algorithm's speed is actually great. This is one of the biggest advantages it provides, even if performance is somewhat sacrificed.

So far, we only focused on supervised machine learning; however, when you work with real datasets, it will not be enough to apply these algorithms by themselves.

Chapter 5: Creating & Accessing Your Python Dictionary

Python dictionaries are usually enclosed by curly brackets { }. However, when accessing and assigning values, square brackets [ ] are used.

To create your own dictionary, you can start with the key 'dict':

dict{ }

dict ['filename'] = ['values']

Example:

dict{ }

dict['name'] = "My name is Billy."

When you print this by running the module with this function:

print dict['name']

The results will appear in a new shell/box – all the values of your dict['name'] will be printed.

See image below:

You could also assign numbers as your dictionary's name, such as dict[1], and so forth. Make sure you have assigned values to your dictionary file.

Example:

dict[1] = "My age is 25."

You can print your dict[1], by using: print dict[1], to display its values/content. See image below:

When you run the module, this will be the result:

Notice that all the values of dict1 have been printed in the results.

If you want to print the complete dictionary, you can use this statement:

print tinydict

But there should be values assigned to your tinydict, or your results will show errors.

See image below:

After you click 'Run', and then 'Run Module', a new shell will appear with results like the image below:

You can also print all the values of your tinydict, by using this statement or code:

print tinydict.values()

The results below will appear:

Notice that there are >>> symbols in this shell. This is because the original shell was used without opening a 'New File'.

If you want to print the keys of your tinydict, you can use this statement:

print tinydict.keys()

When you press 'enter' or execute, the results will be this:

All the keys are printed in the results. Often, the results don't come in the order that it was presented/written in the tinydict.

Reminder:

If you have opted to create a 'New File', click the 'Run', and the 'Run Module'. If not, just press 'enter' and the results will be printed promptly in the same Python shell.

The advantage of creating a 'New File', however, is that you can edit the file without difficulty. This is because when you press the 'enter' key it does not execute the code, not until you click the 'Run' and 'Run Module' menu on the New File's shell, itself.

Accessing Values from a Python Dictionary:

You can access values from a Python dictionary by entering the correct code. To access values, you can use the square brackets and the keyword (key).

In the dictionary, the keyword is separated from its value by a colon (:), and the values are separated by commas, and all items are enclosed in curly braces { }.

Example:

dict={'student': 'White', 'gender': 'female'}

print "dict['student']: ", dict['student']

print "dict['gender']; ", dict['gender']

See image below:

Before you can access this though, the file should have been saved in your device.

Creating and Combining Strings

Writing your strings properly for your codes can help you significantly in obtaining correct results.

These are the steps:

Step #1 – Open a 'New File.'

On this box, you can now create your string.

Step #2 – Identify your variables.

Let's say you have chosen three variables, a, b, and c. You can then assign a string to each of the variables before printing them.

Example:

a=('This is a single quoted string.')

b=("This is a double quoted string.")

c=("""This is a triple quoted string.""")

print (a)

print (b)

print (c)

See the example of composing and assigning values to your variables, using strings, demonstrated in the image below:

Step #3 – Save your New File.

Again, name and 'Save As' your 'New File' where you want it to be. In this case, the file is named string1 and saved in the Python file. Remember to save every time you make changes. See image below.

Step #4 – Run your 'New File'.

You can now run your new Python file by clicking 'Run" and then 'Run Module', or simply key in F5. See image below:

Step #5 – Use your new module (strings 1)

Go back to your Python shell and import your 'New File', strings1, so you can use it. Simply type: import strings1, and then press 'enter'. The results will appear, with your strings displayed quickly.

Let's say you have already assigned the values of string 'a' as 'Remember.' and your string 'b' as "Yesterday and Tomorrow.", you have to save the changes you made to strings1, by clicking 'Save'.

If you want to combine string 'a' and string 'b', you can go back to your Python shell and import strings1, before combining them.

Now, you can combine them, by using the statement or command:

> print (a + b),

and then press 'enter'.

You can do this on your strings1 file itself or in the Python shell. This was done in the file itself, so the combined strings are already displayed when strings1 was imported.

There are other functions that you can take advantage of, such as printing any of the strings repeatedly.

If you want to print string 'b' repeatedly (example: 200 times), you can use the statement: print(b asterisk 200).

> print (b * 200)

This will print your 'b' string = "Yesterday and Tomorrow." 200 times. The long method is using the command:

print (b + b + b ... (until it reaches 200), which is a tedious task. You can enter this function or command in your strings1 file, and then go back to your Python shell and import strings1.

See image below.

The results will be displayed in your shell, when the file (strings1) is imported. See image below.

You can also click 'Run' in your strings1 file to show the results. See image below:

When you click on the 'Run Module' or F5, the same results will appear quickly. See image below:

Reminders:

Generally, you cannot combine arguments that are different.

For example, integers (numbers) and strings (words).

What you can do is to convert your integer into a word-string by using the prefix, 'str'.

You can create a New File to edit you string1 file with a new string.

In this case, I decided to modify the string1 file. Remember always to save your file, every time you edit or create a new file.

Take note that integers don't need any parentheses. You cannot add string literals (words) and numbers in one string, so you have to convert the number to a string first, by the key function: str(b).

Next, add 'a' and 'b' with the function/command +:

print(a + str(b))

Don't forget to enclose your argument in parentheses.

See image below:

Click 'Save', and then click 'Run', and then 'Run Module'.

The combination of arguments 'a' and 'b' will appear, which is:

Remember. 911

See image below:

A more specific example is this.

You want to create a personal file about your clients.

Let's say you have two arguments, 'Names' and 'Ages', that you would like to combine in your file.

The existing data you have are:

Names: Potter Richard, Walker Henry, Fell Don, Dean James

Ages: 20, 34, 41, 32

See image below:

So, if you want to combine the 'Names' and the 'Ages' strings, your code would be:

print (Names + Ages)

Make sure you save, after entering your code. Enclose each entry with quotes, and separate each entry with a comma. Use parentheses (brackets) for word strings, and no parentheses or quotes for integers (numbers). Don't forget the equal sign when assigning your arguments.

Example:

Names = ("Potter Richard", "Walker Henry", "Fell Don", "Dean James")

Ages = 20, 34, 41, 32

print (Names + Ages)

See image below:

Now, save. Click 'Run', and 'Run Module'. See image below:

After you had clicked 'Run Module', a new Python shell will appear displaying the results of your code.

See image below:

In this instance, you don't need to create a name string for your integers.

Using the 'join; ( ) key.

You can also use the key, 'join', to combine strings.

Example:

parts=['Richard', 'Potter', 'Probationary']

> ' '.join(parts)

'Richard Potter Probationary'

> ', '.join(parts)

'Richard, Potter, Probationary'

> ' ' .join(parts)

'Richard Potter Probationary'

See image below:

These are all methods in creating and combining strings.

I hope you can now create your own strings and combine them in your Python shell. Remember is the key functions (+) and 'join'( ).

Accessing and Updating Strings

Python strings are one of the most popular methods in creating and maintaining codes.

You can access your strings promptly by using the keywords (key) 'import'.

When you need to access them, you can simply import them using your Python shell. Simply type:

    import names1,

And then press 'enter'.

See image below:

Of course, you must save your files before you could access them.

For substrings, you can slice through them by using brackets. Anyway, here's one example of accessing your substrings. Let's say your strings are these:

    var1="Welcome to My World."

    var2="Clinical Chemistry"

And you want to get the substrings 1:4 for var1, and the substrings 1:3 for var2. You can enter your statement/code this way: (You can open a 'New File' to do this. Click on 'File', and then 'New File'.

Example:

    var1="Welcome to My World."

    var2="Clinical Chemistry"

    print "var1[1:4]: ",var1[1:4]

    print "var2[1:3]: ",var2[1:3]

See image below:

Keep in mind that just like in your indexes, each letter is assigned a number, with the number starting from o and then onwards.

Hence, for the first variable [var1], letter W=0; letter e = 1, and so forth. For the second variable [var2], the first letter C is equivalent to 0 and then so forth.

When you press 'Run', and then 'Run Module', on your keypads, a new shell will appear with these results. See image below:

If you noticed, only the letters that correspond to the numbers are printed - 'elc' from the original word, 'Welcome to My World'.

W=0,

     e= 1,

     l=2,

     c=3,

     0=4,

     m=5,

     e=6

and so on

Only the letters 'elc' were accessed.

Likewise, with var2, only 'li' was accessed because of the specified numbers – 1:3; in these examples the colon stands for 'to', and #3 is not included in the results. However, only 1 to 2 letters will appear, so the result printed is 'li', from the original word, 'Clinical Chemistry'.

C=0,

    l=1,

    i=2,

    n=3,

    i=4,

    c=5,

    a=6,

    l=7

and so on

Updating your strings

You can update your strings quickly by indicating what updates you want to do. Let's say you want to add the words "Welcome" from your var1 with "Chemistry" from var2, here's how your code/statement would appear:

Example:

    var1="Welcome to My World."

    print "Updated String :- ", var1[:8] + 'Chemistry'

See image below:

When you click 'Run', and then 'Run Module', a new shell will appear with the results:

It's preferable to open a 'New File' every time you input new data, than typing in the original shell, because some beginners may find the results confusing because of the >>> signs. You can also save the 'New File' easily.

See image below:

But if you don't find this confusing, you may opt not to open a 'New File', and type in the new Python shell instead.

See image below:

Chapter 6: Introducing Variables

Variables are one of the key components of any programming language and are what allow us to do all kinds of incredible things with just a few lines of code.

So what is a variable?

Well, if you think back to your high school math, then you may actually recall using variables back then. And variables in Python work in the *exact* same way.

Essentially, a variable is a container or a representative. This is a word or a letter that *represents* a number. That number can change but you can write the letter or word at any point in your math to represent it. You can think of it almost like a box and every time you tell the code to look inside the box, it will find the information you put in there. That means you can change the information regularly (by changing the value of the variable) but Python will still always know where to look!

So if you cast your mind back to your school math days, then you may recall seeing things like this written:

$$10 + x = 13$$

Find x.

In this case, 'x' is actually '3'.

This works in just the same way in Python except there's no 'finding' of x involved. Instead, we're telling Python what x is and then referring to it later. So how do we do this? Pretty simply actually:

    x = 3

We could also say:

    MyVariable = 3

So let's open up the script mode and try using this in part of a little program. Just write:

MyVariable = 3

print(MyVariable)

Now save the program and go to run it. When you do this, you'll find that it simply outputs the value of the variable – which in this case is "3".

We haven't actually explained what 'print' does yet but by now you should have been able to work it out. This is simply a command that writes text to the screen and you can make it anything you want it to be by using quotation marks as we did when we wrote "Hello World".

But you may have noticed that we didn't *need* to use the quotation marks when using the variable. That's because the quotations marks are only there to say 'write this text exactly'.

Integers, Strings and Floats Oh My!

The variable *MyVariable* contains the number 3 with no decimal places. Thus we call it an integer. In other words, we name our variables after the data they contain. So seeing as the number '3.72' is a float, we would call a variable that contained that number a float as well!

So far so easy... But things are about to get significantly more complicated as there are a lot more types of variable and it will pay to at least be familiar with most of these...

The integer and the float are both considered 'number variables'. That means that they contain numerical data.

Actually though, there are also two *more* types of variable. These are the 'long' and the 'complex'. You'll use these two less often but essentially longs are used when you need really long numbers and complexes are used when you need very complex numbers.

So you don't need to worry about that. What you definitely *will* come across in your coding travels though is the 'string'. A string is another type of variable but it isn't numerical. Rather, strings contain letters or words. So a string could be 'a' or it could be 'Adam'. If we say:

MyString = "Hello World!"

print(MyString)

Then the program simply prints 'Hello World!' to the string just like before. Only now we could change the value of 'MyString' and the output would change. This is very helpful when we want to use the same string in lots of places but may need to change the string. For example, we could use a string if we wanted to refer to a user by name in our app. We could assign the name to the string at the start of the app and then easily refer to them using that name elsewhere.

All of the variables we have looked at so far have one thing in common – they hold one piece of data or a single value. There are also other types of variables however that contain *more* than one piece of data. So if we think of our strings, integers and floats as boxes, then these variables are more like filing cabinets, folders or bookshelves.

The standard data types available when using Python then are:

☐ Numbers

- Integers
- Floats
- Longs
- Complexes

☐ Strings

☐ Lists

☐ Tuples

☐ Dictionaries

For now you don't need to learn about lists, tuples and dictionaries but if you just can't wait then skip ahead to the called 'Advanced Variables'.

Performing Operations on Variables

Remember how we said that variables allowed our programs to change? That's because we can change the value of the variable whenever we like throughout our code.

As we've already seen, we can set the value of a variable very simply like so at the start of our code:

MyNumber = 3

But if we later want to change the value of our number we can simply change it *again* later on. For example:

MyNumber = 3

print(MyNumber)

MyNumber = 4

print(MyNumber)

If you run this program then it will simply output '3' and then '4'. Like so:

But likewise, we can also change our variables using the very same operations that we used in 4. For example:

MyNumber1 = 3

MyNumber2 = 4

```
MyNumber3 = MyNumber1 + MyNumber2

print(MyNumber3)
```

Can you guess what this will output?

Or how about:

```
MyNumber1 = 3 * 2

MyNumber2 = 4

MyNumber1 = MyNumber2 – 3

MyNumber3 = MyNumber1 + MyNumber2

print(MyNumber3)
```

You can even let a variable refer to itself. For example, what do you think this line of code does:

```
MyNumber1 = MyNumber1 + 1
```

Essentially, this increases *MyNumber1* by '1'. So you are saying that the value of the variable will become whatever it is right now *plus* one.

Right now this might all seem a little strange but as we go through and look at the different commands you can use in Python it should start to make a lot more sense!

The next question you might be wondering is whether or not you can also do this kind of thing with strings? And the good news is that you can and it actually works just the same! Of course you can't *multiply* a string by a string (because that doesn't mean anything!) but what you *can* do is to add two strings together to create a new one. For example:

FirstName = "Bill"

LastName = "Gates"

FullName = FirstName + LastName

print(FullName)

You'll see why all this is important soon!

(Actually, I wasn't being strictly honest when I said you couldn't multiply a string. In fact, writing *FirstName = "Bill" * 10* would make a string with the value "BillBillBillBillBillBillBillBillBillBill"!)

Chapter 7: Naming Conventions and Comments

Variables are one of the most common elements in programming because they allow things to change in a controlled manner – thus allowing for dynamic programs that change over time or in response to input.

One way in which variables are different in other programming languages though, is that they must first be defined. In Python, we can simply say:

x = 3

At any point in our program and then 'x' will be created with the value '3'. In Java though (another popular programming language), x would first have to be created with a statement like:

Int x;

x = 3;

Part of the reason for this is that other programming languages use a much wider range of variables – such a 'Booleans' which can only equal one or zero. Because Python only has a few types of variable, it doesn't need as much structure.

What's also important though is to think carefully when naming your variables. The objective here is to write our code in such a logical and elegant way that a complete stranger could instantly know what it does – that will help if you ever need to collaborate on a project, or if you come back to old code you've written.

When using variables in Python, it's a good idea to use proper case. We've seen that commands like 'print' are normally lower case, so if we use proper case or capitals for our variables, then they will stand out very easily when reading through.

So if you are using a string to refer to a user's name, then what should you call it? A good option would be: *UserName* or *Name*. This will make life much easier than if you call it *Rabbit1112*...

Another tip is to try and choose variables that *read* well as though they were written in English when they're inserted into the code. We'll touch on this more in future.

Using Comments

To make finding your way around just that little bit simpler, note that you can also use comments. 'Comments' are lines of plain English that you can insert into your code. The compiler will ignore these lines when you run your program but it means you can add instructions, notes and references for yourself or other members of your team.

To insert a comment, simply precede your line with a '#' symbol. The comment will then extend to the very end of the physical line. If you're coding using IDLE, then the comment will instantly change to a red font when you get it right:

Think ahead while writing your programs as taking a little time to keep your code clean now can save you a real headache later on!

Chapter 8: Handling Inputs

At the moment, all the programs we've written do is to output information. As you can imagine... this isn't very useful! If you've never written code before, you might even be wondering why any of this matters. After all, if you wanted to say 'Hello World' you could just write it on a piece of paper...

To solve this problem then, we need to start inviting the user to join in and actually interact with the software we've written. One way we can do this is with the command 'input'. The great news is that input is actually very easy to use! Essentially, this just lets the user assign a value to a variable.

So instead of saying:

UserName = "Bill"

You say:

UserName = input("Please enter your name: ")

This now means that the program will add a prompt asking the user to enter their name:

Once the user acquiesces to our request, *UserName* will then equal whatever they said. This means we can say:

UserName = input("Please enter your name: ")

print("Hello " + UserName)

Now, whatever the user says their name is, we can greet them using it! Congratulations are in order: you just created your very first interactive program!

(**Note** that if you're using Python 2, you'll need to use *raw_input* instead of *input*. This is our first example of where Python 2 and Python 3 differ – but it's no biggie!)

So what else can we do with this? Well of course we can also use the input command in order to capture and set other types of data. Such as integers!

For example:

UserAge = input("Please enter your age: ")

print("You are ", int(UserAge))

In this example there are a couple of other things going on but you can probably work out some of it.

First of all, we're creating a string called *UserAge* just as we did before. The 'prompt' is asking for the age and input will automatically be converted into an string.

From there, we are then printing the output. Note that we can't use '+' when adding a string to an integer, so instead we're just using a common to list both values one after the other.

And next, we are converting the value that user gave us into a string by using the *int(UserAge)* line. You can also convert integers into strings by saying *str(Number)*. This way you could convert 4 into "4".

Let's have a bit more fun and see what we can do with this information and a little math...

```
UserAge = input("How old are you? ")

print(int(UserAge), "is sooo old!")

YearsTo100 = 100 - int(UserAge)

print("In ", YearsTo100, "years, you'll be a hundred!!")
```

Now you have a program that is basically very rude about your age and that tells you how many years until you're 100. Nice!

Or what if we take it one step further?

```
UserAge = input("How old are you? ")

print(int(UserAge), "is sooo old!")

YearsTo100 = 100 - int(UserAge)

print("In ", YearsTo100, "years, you'll be a hundred!!")

print("That is ", int(UserAge) * 360, " days! Or ", (int(UserAge) * 360) * 24, " hours. Man...")
```

That extra line means it can now tell us how many hours and days we've been alive. I'm 28, which I'm informed is 10,080 days or 241,920 hours.

The program might be a little offensive... but it's also starting to pull together quite a few different things we've learned! At this point we're able to accept input to create new variables, then perform operations with those variables and present an answer on the screen!

Loops

Input is one of the most useful operations you'll find yourself using at first when you program. But this is still only scratching the surface of what you'll be able to do as you learn more and more Python.

Another powerful tool for instance is to use loops. Loops essentially allow a piece of code to keep running and repeating itself.

There are two different types of loops, which operate based on different conditions. One of the most common examples of a loop for example is the 'While' loop. The clue as to how this loop works is very much in the name. Basically, a while loop runs *while* something is true.

So for instance, we could say:

Number = 0

while Number < 100:

    Number = Number + 1

    print("Counted to", Number)

All this would then do is to print numbers from 0-100 on the screen. The *while* command is followed by a conditional statement (*Number < 100*) and everything that follows the colon and is indented will then happen while that loop runs. If we remove the indentation, then this signifies that we have come to the end of the loop. So the final line in this section of code will only show once the loop has completed:

```
Number = 0
while Number < 100:
    Number = Number + 1
    print("Counted to ", Number)
print("Finished and counted to 100")
```

Leaving a space between the lines makes no difference.

This is another situation where it becomes *very* important to be careful with formatting and planning. Simply pressing backspace and accidentally deleting an indentation is enough to prevent the code from working properly! This is quite different to other types of code such as java or C# where the loops are contained within curly brackets *{like this}*.

Note that if we hadn't included the line *Number = Number + 1* then the loop would have run forever!

The other type of loop we can use is the 'For' loop. For basically performs some kind of counting job and finishes once that job is over. For example, this:

```
for Counting in range(100):
    print(Counting)
```

Does the same thing that the previous loop did – counts to one hundred! But we could also do something else interesting – for example we could do this:

for Counting in range(10, 100):

    print(Counting)

And thereby count from 10 to 100!

This is another example of something that might seem rather pointless currently. Why would you want to count to 100 this way when you have other methods? Well, one example might be to look through a list of items.

What else can you do with loops? Well, one option is to 'break' the loop. This simply terminates the loop early and then continues with the rest of the program. This can be used in the 'while' and 'for' loops and is something we'll come across later on...

One way that it might be useful as an example though, is if we use *while True*. This statement (notice the capital 'True') simply runs our loop until we say otherwise with *break*.

Another one that will come in handy is 'continue'. This works similarly to the 'break' statement, except that it simply begins the loop again from the start. And if you were 'For' loop, then the condition that you were testing would also be reset. Again, it will all make perfect sense soon...

Chapter 9: Working with the Conditional Statements

There are going to be times when you will work on a program in Python where you will need the program to make some decisions for you, without you being there to tell it how to answer each response that it gets. You can set up the conditions that need to be met to help out with this but there is a lot of unknown when the user is allowed to add in any input that they want, and the conditional statements are going to help you learn how to do this. Since you are not able to handle or guess all of the answers or inputs that the user may give, and so these conditional statements are going to be there to help you get things done.

You will find that these conditional statements are going to be a bit different than what you are used to, but they can work on a lot of different programs that you try to write. They are simple, but it is easy to add to them and change things up so that you are able to get more done, and you can handle any of the answers that your users decide to use

When it comes to working with these conditional statements, there are going to be three options that you are able to work with. These are the if statement, the elif statement, and the if else statement. These are all important, but they are going to work in slightly different ways in order to help you to get some of the codings that you want to be done. Let's explore how each of these is going to work inside your own code.

Starting with the if statement

Out of the conditional statements, the most basic of the three and the one that we are going to focus on first is going to be the if statement. The if statement is a basic conditional statement, and sometimes is going to seem too simple to use on a regular basis. In fact, it is more common that you are going to work with the if else statement or the elif statement when in this kind of field, but it is still important to learn how to work with the if statement so that we get some of the basics that come with this kind of conditional statement:

You can probably already guess that this will cause some problems with most codes, but it is still important to know how to use these statements. A simple code that you can work with for these conditional statements include:

```
age = int(input("Enter your age:"))

if (age <=18):

print("You are not eligible for voting, try next election!")

print("Program ends")
```

There are a few things that will show up with this code. If you have a user go to the program and state that their age is under 18, then the program will work and display the message that is listed there. The user can read this message and then end the program right there.

Now one thing to notice here is that there is a chance for things to not go as planned when you are working with this kind of code. If the user wants to put in an answer for their age that is 18 or higher, then the code is not set up at this point to handle this issue. Right now, the program is going to only list out the message that you have when the user puts their age in as something under 18. But if they wrote out their age as something higher, then it is not going to meet up with the conditions that you have, and nothing will happen.

Of course, we do not want to have a code where only one answer is right, at least now when it comes to the age of the person using the program. They want to be able to put in their real age at the time, and this may or may not be below 18. You want to make sure that your program is working the way that you want, and this is why we will move on to the if else statements.

Moving on to the if else statements

While the if statements are a good place to get some practice when it comes to writing your own codes in Python, there are not going to be a ton of times in programming when you would want to use these at all. It is likely that you don't want to leave the screen empty with nothing there for the user to see. And this is why we want to learn how to work with the if else statement to handle the issues from above.

The if else statement is going to take the things that we have looked at in the if statement, but moves them along another step so they make more sense and can handle more situations. With the example that we had worked on before, the user is going to be able to see the message we had before if they put in any age under 18. But then this goes a bit further because it is also going to provide us with a message if the user is older than 18 as well. This if else statement is going to make sure that the user is going to get some kind of message, no matter what age they put into the system at the time.

With the voting example that we had above, you can implement the following code to make an if else statement:

```
age = int(input("Enter your age:"))

if (age <=18):

print("You are not eligible for voting, try next election!")

else

print("Congratulations! You are eligible to vote. Check out your local polling station to find out more information!)

print("Program ends")
```

With this option, you are adding in the else statement, which will cover every age that doesn't fall under 18. This way, if the user does list that as their age, something will still pull up on the screen for them. This can provide you with more freedom when working on your code and you can even add in a few more layers to this. If you want to divide it up so that you get four or five age groups and each one gets a different response, you simply need to add in more if statements to make it happen. The else statement is at the end to catch everything else.

We can take this a bit further to see how things go. Let's say that we want to create a code using the if else statement in order to ask our users what their favorite color is. You would continue on with the if statements based on the colors you would like to choose. You are not able to list out all of the colors that are available because this would take forever and be hard to work on but maybe you choose five colors and give them if statements with a message that is attached.

Then, if the user doesn't pick one of those five colors that you put an if statement with, it will be caught by the else statement as well. This ensures that all answers are caught and responded to, without having to worry about listing out and guessing all of the different possibilities that the user can put in.

Finishing it out with the elif statements

Now that we have had some time to explore a bit with the if statement and the if else statement, it is time to take a look at how the elif statement is going to be the same or different, and how you can use it in your code. You will find that these add in a different kind of level to the codes that you are writing, but they still have ease of use to them.

It is possible to write in as many of the elif statements as you would like to the code, and then you also need to add in the else statement, as we did above with the if else statement, to cover any of the other decisions that need to be handled in the code. You can think of the elif statement like something similar to some of the older games out there, the ones that had a menu of options and allowed the user to pick from one of these. This is pretty similar to how we are going to set up our elif statements.

When you are working on these elif statements, you are able to add in as many different options as you would like to finish it up. Sometimes, you may just add one, two, or three, but you are not limited by this and can add in as many as you would like. Keep in mind though that the more elif statements that you add into the code, the messier it gets and the more that you have to write out. To see how the coding for the elif statements is going to work, make sure to check out the following code:

Print("Let's enjoy a Pizza! Ok, let's go inside Pizzahut!")

print("Waiter, Please select Pizza of your choice from the menu")

pizzachoice = int(input("Please enter your choice of Pizza:"))

if pizzachoice == 1:

print('I want to enjoy a pizza napoletana')

elif pizzachoice == 2:

```
print('I want to enjoy a pizza rustica')

elif pizzachoice == 3:

print('I want to enjoy a pizza capricciosa')

else:

print("Sorry, I do not want any of the listed pizza's, please bring
a Coca Cola for me.")
```

With this option, the user is able to choose the type of pizza they want to enjoy, but you can use the same syntax for anything you need in your code. If the user pushes the number 2 in the code, they are going to get a pizza Rustica. If they don't like any of the options, then they are telling the program that they just want to have something to drink, in this case, a Coca Cola.

This is a simple way to use elif statements to give the user a set of choices. In the other options, the user could add in any choice that they wanted, but in the elif statement, they can either pick that they want one of the choices that you provide, or they will have to go with the default option at the end. This can work well for many games that you may want to pick, for some tests online, and other programs where you want to limit the choices that the user gets to pick from in the code.

As you can see, there are a lot of different things that you are able to do when working on these conditional statements. You are able to choose what conditions you would like to have in place, and then make sure that the program is going to behave in the right way the whole time. You can choose whether the if statement, the if else statement or the elif statement is going to be the right one for you, and then add these to the code that you are writing.

Chapter 10: Exception Handling in the Python Language

The next topic that we need to spend some time exploring in this guidebook is the idea of exception handling. There are going to be times when your code tries to show up some errors or other problem inside the code that you are doing, and this is where the exception is going to occur. Knowing when to recognize these exceptions, how to handle them, and even how to make some of your own can make a big difference in how well you are able to do some of your own coding in Python.

These exceptions are going to be brought up by the compiler in a lot of different situations, and sometimes, they are going to look like a simple error message like you may have seen on your own computer before. It is important to really read through any of these exceptions that come up in your code and read through them so that you can learn what they are about, and how you can handle them properly at the same time. This isn't meant to be something to scare you, but there are things that you can do to handle these exceptions and to make sure that you are going to be able to handle them in the proper manner.

Now, there are going to be a few exceptions that are already recognized inside the library that you are using in Python. If you want to write out a code with them in there, or if you find that the user is trying to do something that isn't proper for your program, then the compiler is going to send out an exception about this in order to get it to stop. In some cases, the program you are writing is going to need some extra limitations in place to handle it, and you can raise up, after creating, your own exception.

A good example of an exception that your compiler is automatically going to raise up is when you or the user is to divide it by zero. The compiler is then going to recognize that this is something the user is not able to do, and it is going to send out that exception as an alert. It can also be something that is going to be called up if you, as the programmer, are trying to call up a function and the name is not spelled in the proper manner so there is no match present to bring up.

There are a few different exceptions that are automatically found in your Python library. It is a good idea to take some time to look through them and recognize these exceptions so you can recognize them later on. Some of the most common exceptions that you need to worry about include:

Finally—this is the action that you will want to use to perform cleanup actions, whether the exceptions occur or not.

Assert—this condition is going to trigger the exception inside of the code

Raise—the raise command is going to trigger an exception manually inside of the code.

Try/except—this is when you want to try out a block of code and then it is recovered thanks to the exceptions that either you or the Python code raised.

Raising an Exception

The first thing that we need to take a look at, now that we know a bit more about these exceptions and what they mean, is how to write one out, and some of the steps that you can use if one of these does end up in your own code. If you are going through some of the code writing, and you start to notice that an exception will be raised, know that often the solution is going to be a simple one. But as the programmer, you need to take the time to get this fixed. To help us get started here, let's take a look at what the syntax of the code for raising an exception is all about.

x = 10

y = 10

result = x/y #trying to divide by zero

print(result)

The output that you are going to get when you try to get the interpreter to go through this code would be:

>>>

Traceback (most recent call last):

File "D: \Python34\tt.py", line 3, in <module>

result = x/y

ZeroDivisionError: division by zero

>>>

As we take a moment to look at the example that we have here, we can see that the program is going to bring up an exception for us, mainly because we are trying to divide a number by zero and this is something that is not allowed in the Python code (and any other coding language for that matter). If you decide not to make any changes at this point, and you go ahead and run the program as it is, you could end up with the compiler sending you an error message. The code is going to tell the user the problem, but as you can see, the problem is not listed out in an easy-to-understand method and it is likely the user will have no idea what is going on or how they can fix the problem at all.

With that example that we worked on above, you have some options. You can choose to leave the message that is kind of confusing if you don't know any coding, or you can add in a new message that is easier to read and explains why this error has been raised in the first place. It won't have a lot of numbers and random letters that only make sense to someone who has done coding for a bit, which makes the whole thing a bit more user-friendly overall. The syntax that you can use to control the message that your user is going to see includes:

```
x = 10

y = 0

result = 0

try:

result = x/y

print(result)

except ZeroDivisionError:

print("You are trying to divide by zero.")
```

Take a look at the two codes above. The one that we just did looks a little bit similar to the one above it, but this one has a message inside. This message is going to show up when the user raises this particular exception. You won't get the string of letters and numbers that don't make sense, and with this one, the user will know exactly what has gone wrong and can fix that error.

Can I define my own exceptions?

In the examples above, we took some time to define and handle the exceptions that the compiler offered to us and are already found in the Python library. Now it is time for us to take it a bit further and learn how to raise a few of our own exceptions in any kind of code that we want to write. Maybe you are working on a code that only allows for a few choices to the user, one that only allows them to pick certain numbers or one that only allows them to have so many chances at guessing. These are common things that we see when we work with gaming programs but can work well in other programs that you design.

When you make these kinds of exceptions, the compiler is going to have to be told that an exception is being raised, because it is not going to see that there is anything wrong in this part of the code. The programmer has to go in and let the compiler know what rules it has to follow, and what exceptions need to be raised in the process. A good example of the syntax that you can use to make this happen in your own code will be below:

```
class CustomException(Exception):

def_init_(self, value):

self.parameter = value

def_str_(self):
return repr(self.parameter)

try:

raise CustomException("This is a CustomError!")

except CustomException as ex:

print("Caught:", ex.parameter)
```

In this code, you have been successful in setting up your own exceptions and whenever the user raises one of these exceptions, the message of "Caught: This is a CustomError!" is going to come up on the screen. This is the best way to show your users that you have added in a customer exception into the program, especially if this is just one that you personally created for this part of the code, and not one that the compiler is going to recognize on its own.

Just like with the other examples that we went through, we worked with some generic wording just to show how exceptions are able to work. You can easily go through and change this up so that you get a message that is unique for the code that you are writing and will explain to the user what is going on when they get the error message to show up.

Learning how to work with some of the exceptions that can come up in your code is one of the best ways to make sure that your codes work the way that you want, that the user is going to like working with your program, and that everything is going to proceed as normal and do what you want. Take some time to practice these examples and see how they can work for you in order to handle any of the exceptions that come up in your code.

Chapter 11: Functions, Classes and Methods

This methodology allows us to create objects that will contain data, together with various attributes and methods that describe it or perform an action on it. Therefore, you can say that a Python object is nothing more than a collection of data types and some parameters that describe them or give them additional functionality.

In this chapter you will be introduced to the concept of object oriented programming. You will learn the basics behind the methodology and learn how to define a class and a method.

Introduction to OOP

Objects are built into classes of objects and then we apply a number of methods which will affect anything that belongs to a class. The theory might start sounding a bit confusing because we started exploring the slightly more advanced programming notions, but look at it this way.

Imagine you have a certain car and you define it as a class. The car, just like the class, has a number of attributes and behaviors that are described. In the case of your car, these attributes will be the brand, model, fuel type, color, number of seats, year, etc. The behavior is described by a method which belongs to the class. Since this is a car, you will probably have a start, accelerate, and stop method at least. Now that the car class is defined, we can build a number of objects that will have all of these attributes and methods in common. Let's say you will have a Mercedes as your first object and its attributes will describe the fact that it runs on diesel fuel and that it was manufactured in 2017. Since the Mercedes is a car, it will share the same methods as the car class. It can start, accelerate, and stop. Next, you can create another car object that shares the same information. As you can see, object oriented programming makes it much easier to create something with a lot less code. You don't have to define everything again and again. All you need is the schematic for the class and then create derivative objects that share various features with the parent class.

Now let's get back to a little more theory before putting everything into practice. Keep in mind that object oriented programming is something that you will have to eventually master because you cannot create powerful and efficient applications without it. With that being said, there are four major principles behind OOP:

1. Encapsulation: This concept refers to locking an object within a private class. The fact that the class is private means that other objects will no longer have any kind of access to the objects inside that specific class. Encapsulation is used mostly for security purposes so that you do not change sensitive objects

on purpose or by accident when working with other public objects.

2. Abstraction: Maintaining complex programs always requires a great deal of dedication from a programmer or even several. However, by following the abstraction rules we can make everything easier. Information about objects is often sealed because it is considered unnecessary. You don't need to know all the details in order to perform an operation. This means that for the purpose of code maintenance you want to gain access only to what is relevant to an object or several if they are related. For instance, abstraction let's you have access only to how to drive your car. You don't need to know about all the internal mechanisms that are processed by the engine and other mechanical components.

3. Inheritance: This is one of the most powerful concepts and why object oriented programming is the software development standard. Let's say you create a large number of objects. Some of them are bound to share some common attributes and methods, even if they aren't identical. Instead of writing the same methods again and again, you can extract them from one of the objects and apply it to another one. Furthermore, you can create new classes using other classes. For instance, you can

have a parent class from which a number of child classes derive and share various features. All of this can form a hierarchy where a child class will use the base logic provided by the parent class, together with any new functionality you create specifically for the child class. This way you can reuse code and features instead of writing them several times.

4. Polymorphism: Typing the same code multiple times is not a good idea. You waste time and resources. This is what polymorphism is for. You can create an object that comes in several forms. Then you can let Python decide which version should be executed based on a number of parameters. This concept allows you to write short, clean, and efficient code.

Object oriented programming is at the heart of the standard software development cycle. You may be a beginner and you won't benefit from this methodology just yet, however, you need to explore it and learn it in order to master Python programming. Now, let's get back to coding.

Functions

Before you learn how to define basic classes and methods, you should learn how to use functions. Functions don't belong necessarily to the object oriented programming paradigm, however, they do solve many beginner problems and mistakes and you should learn how to use them before constructing classes.

There is no real rule about writing the same code block multiple times in the same program or script. It will all work just fine. However, you will have more lines of code to deal with, plus your program will probably need more time and resources to process everything. Therefore, it is generally accepted that if you need to write the same code more than twice, you should go back and turn everything into a function.

Functions allow you to write any statements and instructions you need, but once. Then you give that code block a name and turn it into a function. Whenever you need to use that code again, you simply call the function by its name instead of writing all the statements again. Here's how to write a basic function:

def myfunction():

print("This is my function!")

Functions are defined by using the "def" keyword, followed by the name of the function and two parantheses that can contain a number of parameters. Once the function is defined, you call it like this:

myFunction()

You can call it as often as needed. Now, we mentioned parameters. Inside the parentheses of a function, you can establish some information. A parameter is simply a variable that becomes part of the function definition. Here's an example:

```
def myName(firstname):

print(firstname + " Smith")

myName("John")

myName("James")

myName("Jonah")
```

As you can see we have one parameter passed to our function. When we make the function call, it will print the parameter together with anything else. Keep in mind that functions can have one parameter, multiple parameters, or no parameters. If you define more than one, simply separate them with the use of a comma. Next, let's create a default setting for our function with a set parameter which will always be called if we do not use any other parameter. Here's how this looks in code:

```
def myFunction(country = "Germany"):

print ("I am from " + country)

myFunction("China")

myFunction("France")

myFunction()

myFunction("Italy")
```

The result should look something like this:

I am from China

I am from France

I am from Germany

I am from Italy

Notice that the third time we called the function alone without mentioning any parameter. In this case, the default parameter we defined in the beginning is used.

The functions you created so far don't really create any values for us to use in a program. All they do is something that we instructed them to do. You will rarely if ever use such functions. You need values in order to assign them to a variable and then use the variable for other operations. Let's define a function and return a value with it by using the return keyword:

```
def myFunction(x):

return 10 * x

print(myFunction(2))

print(myFunction(5))
```

Now that you have the basics down, you can use functions to simplify your code and write fewer confusing lines. Next, you will learn how to use classes and methods in order to further refine your code.

How to Define a Class

Classes are at the heart of object oriented programming. Let's see the syntax and then discuss it:

```
class Person:

def _init_(self, name, tel):
```

```
self.name = name
```

```
self.tel = tel
```

In this example, however, all we did was define a class without any objects in it. However, take note that we have used a constructor method during the definition of the class. This method is used by adding the "_init" attachment to the definition. Its purpose is to be used when we create a different instance of our class.

In the next line we have another important keyword which is specific to Python. The "self" keyword is needed whenever we create a method inside the class. If you are familiar with other programming languages, you will notice that the concept is similar to using the keyword "this". The purpose of this keyword in our example is to declare a variable which can be used by any objects that belong to the same class. Now, let's create an instance of our class:

```
p = Person ("Smith", "123321")
```

```
p.name
```

Now we have a new object called Smith, which belongs to the person class. That's it. Even though this is a basic example, you can now create simple classes and variations of classes and then call them as needed throughout your code. They work similarly to functions in a way. Once you declare all the details about a class, you simply call it later in your code whenever you want to perform an action on it.

How to Define a Method

Methods are essentially functions that are attached to a class or an object that belongs to a class. It can only be applied to them when we call it and it is also isolated from any other data that is outside of a class. For instance, you can have methods with the same name, but if they are attached to different classes that are isolated from each other there will be no conflict between them.

Here's a simple example:

```
class Pet (object):

def my_method(self):

print ("This is a dog")

dog = Pet()

dog.my_method()
```

What we have here is a pet class that contains a dog object. You will notice that we call the method in the last line by specifying its attachment to the object.

Chapter 12: Using Linear Regression for Predictions

Linear regression has to be one of the most common of all statistical techniques, being a study of additive and linear relationships between variables. Many different industries use linear regression to create models to help their businesses. Take the retail sector, for example. There are multiple factors that affect a product's sale, such as price, seasonal, promotions and so on.

The use of linear regression can help a business to understand how these factors influence sales and to calculate what the baseline sales are – how many sales of a product there are should there be no external factors. In this chapter, you will be creating a simple linear regression model and a multiple regression model.

Simple Linear Regression

Simple linear regression has just one variable and we can describe it with the following formula:

$y = A + Bx$

The independent variable is x and the dependent is y, the intercept is A (x to the power of zero) and the coefficient to B. The dataset in use will have information relating to the weight in KG and height in cm of a sample of men:

```
>>> import numpy as np

>>> import pandas as pd

>>> from scipy import stats

>>> import matplotlib.pyplot as plt

>>> sl_data =
pd.read_csv('Data/Mens_height_weight.csv')

>>> fig, ax = plt.subplots(1, 1)

>>> ax.scatter(sl_data['Height'],sl_data['Weight'])

>>> ax.set_xlabel('Height')

>>> ax.set_ylabel('Weight')

>>> plt.show()
```

From the resulting plot, you can see that the linear relationship between height and weight of each individual is evident.

We can see the correlation between the variables like this:

```
>>> sl_data.corr()
```

The correlation matrix that results from this is:

HeightWeight

Height1.0000000.942603

Weight0.9426031.000000

From this, we can see that the correlation between height and weight is based on the value coefficient of 0.94 from the Pearson correlation which has a range of -1 to +1; the more positive a number, the stronger the relationship between variable where they increase/decrease together. If there is a negative value, the relationship is still strong but goes the opposite direction.

Using weight as a dependent variable and x as independent, we can generate a linear regression model:

```
>>># Create linear regression object
>>> lm = linear_model.LinearRegression()
>>># Train model using training sets
>>> lm.fit(sl_data.Height[:,np.newaxis],
sl_data.Weight)
>>> print 'Intercept is ' + str(lm.intercept_) + '\n'
Intercept is -99.2772096063
>>> print 'Coefficient value of height is ' +
str(lm.coef_) + '\n'
Coefficient value of height is [ 1.00092142]
>>> print pd.DataFrame(zip(sl_data.columns,lm.coef_),
columns = ['features', 'estimatedCoefficients'])
```

In that code, linear_model.LinearRegression() was used to create lm, a linear regression object. The fit() method for lm was then used for defining the dependent and independent variable; in this case, weight is dependent and height is independent. lm.intercept_ was used to get the intercept value an lm.coef for the coefficient. The final code line helps to create a DataFrame of the independent and all the coefficients that correspond to it. This will become far more useful when we move onto multiple regression.

Next, the scatter chart can be plotted with a trend line:

>>> fig, ax = plt.subplots(1, 1)

>>> ax.scatter(sl_data.Height,sl_data.Weight)

>>>

ax.plot(sl_data.Height,lm.predict(sl_data.Height[:, np.newaxis]),

color = 'red')

>>> ax.set_xlabel('Height')

>>> ax.set_ylabel('Weight')

>>> plt.show()

Multiple Regression

Multiple linear regression is when we use two or more independent variables for predicting the dependent variable:

$Y'=a+b_1x_1+b_2x_2+ ..... +b_nx_n$

Breaking this formula down, the dependent variable is Y, the intercept is a, the coeffiicents are b1 and b2 and the independent variables are x1 and x2. Note also that when the dependent variable is squared, it is still linear; if we have a sqaured coefficient, it becomes nonlinear.

We're going to build our multiple linear regression model using the NBA basketball dataset for predicting the average points per game. The column descriptions are:

- height – height in feet

- weight – weight in pounds

- success_field_goals – percentage of field goals successful out of 100 attempts

- success_free_throws – percentage of free throws successful out of 100 attempts

- avg_points_scored – average scored points per game

The code below takes this data and the DataFrame's describe() method is used to obtain each field's univariate metrics:

```
>>> b_data = pd.read_csv('Data/basketball.csv')
>>> b_data.describe()
```

The output from that is:

heightweight   success_field_goals   success_free _throws   avg_points_scored

count54.00000054.000000   54.000000   54.000000
            54.000000
mean6.587037209.907407   0.449111   0.741852
            11.790741

std 0.458894 30.265036 0.056551 0.100146 5.899257

min 5.700000 105.000000 0.291000 0.244000 2.800000

25% 6.225000 185.000000 0.415250 0.713000 8.150000

50% 6.650000 212.500000 0.443500 0.753500 10.750000

75% 6.900000 235.000000 0.483500 0.795250 13.600000

max 7.600000 263.000000 0.599000 0.900000 27.400000

This table gives us a better understanding of the data and the ability to make these observations:

- On average, a basketball player is about 6 ft. 5-inches tall

- The shortest player is 5 ft. 7-inches

- The tallest player comes in at 7 ft. 7-inches

- The lightest player weighs 105 pounds

- The heaviest weighs 263 pounds

- The best individual field goal percentage is 60%

- The worst individual field goal percentage is 29%

- Average field goal attempt is 45%, but there is a small standard deviation which tells us that the majority of players show a percentage of 40 to 50%

- With the free throws, one player misses 0.75% of the time

- The best player at free throws has a success rate of 90%

- Most players have a free throw success percentage of 70 to 80%

- Highest score by a player per game is 27

- Lowest score is 3

- Average score per player is 12 points

To see the variable correlation:

```
>>> b_data.corr()
```

	height	weight	success_field_goals	success_free_throws	avg_points_scored
height	1.000000	0.834324	0.495546	-0.259271	-0.068906
weight	0.834324	1.000000	0.516021	-0.290159	-0.009844

success_field_goals	0.495546	0.516051	1.000000	-0.018570
	0.338760			
success_free_throws	-0.259271	-0.290159	-0.018570	1.000000
	0.244852			
avg_points_scored	-0.068906	-0.009844	0.338760	0.244852
	1.000000			

From this table we can deduce this:

- Height and weight has a high correlation

- Successful field goals shows a weak positive correlation in terms of weight and height

- Average points scored seems to show the most correlation with success_field_goals even though they are not correlated highly

Now let's see how each independent variable is distributed in respect of the independent variable:

```
>>> fig, ax = plt.subplots(1, 1)
>>> ax.scatter(b_data.height,
b_data.avg_points_scored)
>>> ax.set_xlabel('height')
>>> ax.set_ylabel('Average points scored per game')
>>> plt.show()
```

In the resulting scatter plot, it is easy to see that the height and average points scored do not show a clear pattern; instead, we get a random distribution.

Looking at the distribution between weight and average points scored:

```
>>> fig, ax = plt.subplots(1, 1)
>>> ax.scatter(b_data.weight,
b_data.avg_points_scored)
>>> ax.set_xlabel('weight')
>>> ax.set_ylabel('Average points scored per game')
>>> plt.show()
```

From the result, it looks like 105 pounds could be an outlier; it also shows a lower average score. The players who weigh in at nearly 240 pounds show the most variation in score so we can make a hypothesis that heavier and taller players have bigger scores while shorter, heavier players have the lower scores.

The distribution between average points scored and successful field goals:

```
>>> fig, ax = plt.subplots(1, 1)
>>> ax.scatter(b_data.success_field_goals,
b_data.avg_points_scored)
>>> ax.set_xlabel('success_field_goals')
>>> ax.set_ylabel('Average points scored per game')
```

```
>>> plt.show()
```

The result shows some linear relationship between success_field_goals and average points scored but we still get a highly scattered distribution.

Chapter 13: Replacing and Correcting words

When we are working with text, we will normally come across the incorrect text. Such text needs to be corrected. In NLP, there are numerous through which we can do this. Let us discuss them.

Converting Text to Lowercase

Once you get your text, it may be necessary for you to convert it into lowercase. This is possible in Python. We only have to call the *lower() function* provided by Python on our text and it will convert it into lowercase.

The following example demonstrates this:

myString = "The 5 countries include China, United States, Indonesia, India,and Brazil."

str = myString.lower()

print(str)

The code will return the following upon execution:

We have created a string of text and assigned it to the variable *myString*. We have then created the variable *str* and assigned it to the output of the operation where the above string is converted to lowercase. The value of this string has then been printed on the console.

If you want to work with the text while in uppercase, you can call the *upper() function* on it as demonstrated below:

myString = "The 5 countries include China, United States, Indonesia, India, and Brazil."

str = myString.upper()

print(str)

The code should return the following output upon execution:

Removing Numbers

In some cases, you may not want to work with numbers in your analysis. This means that they should be removed from the text. This can be done in Python using regular expressions. Consider the example given below:

import re

myString = 'Box A has 4 red and 6 white balls, while Box B has 3 red and 5 blue balls.'

output = re.sub(r'\d+', '', myString)

print(output)

We have begun by importing the *re* library. This is the library that allows us to work with regular expressions in Python.

We have then defined a variable named *myString* and assigned it to a string with combined words and numbers. We have then called the *sub() method* provided by the re library to help us in substituting the integers. The *output* of this operation has been assigned to the variable named *output*. We have then printed the value of this variable on the console. The code will give the following result upon execution:

The above output shows that the numbers have been removed from the text. You can now work with your text without numbers.

Removing Punctuation

You may want to remove a number of symbols from your text for easy processing. Examples of such symbols include #, $, %, *, & (), +, -, ., /, :, ;, <=>, ?, @, [, \,], ^, _, `, {, |, }, ~,]. Python provides us with a way of doing this.

The following code demonstrates this:

```
import string
```

myString = "This &is [a] string? {with} many. punctuation.? marks!!!!"

output   =   myString.translate(string.maketrans("",""), string.punctuation)

print(output)

The code will remove all the punctuation marks from the string.

Removing Whitespace

You may want to work with text without leading and ending spaces. You can do away with these from your text by calling the *strip()* method. Here is an example:

myString = " \t a sample string\t "

str = myString.strip()

print(str**)**

We have defined a string and assigned it to the variable *myString*. this string has some whitespaces created by the \t *option (tab)*. We have then invoked the *strip() function* on the string and assigned the output to the variable str. We have then printed the value of this variable to the console. The code gives the following result:

Part of Speech Tagging (POS)

The goal of POS is to assign the various parts of a speech to every word of the provided text like nouns, adjectives, verbs, etc. This is normally done based on the definition and the context.

There are various tools that provide us with POS taggers, including *NLTK, TextBlob,* etc. In this case, we will use *TextBlob* to demonstrate this. To install this library, run the following command on the terminal of your operating system:

pip3 install textblob

This should install the library. It should run quickly because you have already installed *NLTK*. After that, run the following code that demonstrates how speech tagging can be done:

from textblob import TextBlob

import nltk

nltk.download('averaged_perceptron_tagger')

myString = "Parts of speech: an article, to run, fascinating, quickly, and, of"

output = TextBlob(myString)

print(output.tags)

The code should return the following output:

As you have noticed, each word in the text has been assigned to its right tag. This is because we invoked the *TextBlob() function* and passed the name of our string to it. The output was then printed on the console.

Named entity Recognition

The purpose of named entity recognition in NLP is to identify the named entities in a set of text and assign them into the predefined categories such as locations, organizations, names of individuals, etc.

Let us demonstrate how this can be done using the nltk *package:*
import nltk

from nltk import word_tokenize, pos_tag, ne_chunk

nltk.download('maxent_ne_chunker')

nltk.download('words')

myString = "He worked for Microsoft and attended a conference in Italy"

print(ne_chunk(pos_tag(word_tokenize(myString))))

The code should give the result given below upon execution:

We began by importing the *nltk* library and a number of functions from the same library. The necessary packages needed for named entity recognition, in this case, have been downloaded. We have then created a variable named *myString* and assigned a string to it. The functions have then been invoked on the string. The code will return the result given below upon execution:

Collocation Extraction

Collocations refer to words that occur together more frequently that it would happen by chance. Examples of collocations include *"free time"*, *"break the rules"*, *"by the way"*, *"keep in mind"*, *"get ready"* and many others. The following code demonstrates how these can be identified using *ICE*.

To install this module, run the following command:

pip3 install ICE

The command should install the package successfully. Now run the following command:

import ICE import CollocationExtractor

input=["she and Charlse duel with all keys on the line."]

extractor   =
CollocationExtractor.with_collocation_pipeline("T1" , bing_key
= "Temp",pos_check = False)

print(extractor.get_collocations_of_length(input, length = 3))

Finding Synonyms

We will use *wordnet,* which is an NLTK corpus reader, an English lexical database. We can use it to determine the meaning of a word, antonym or synonym. It can be defined as a semantically oriented English dictionary.

To import it from *nltk* corpus into our work space, we run the following command:

from nltk.corpus import wordnet

Synset is one of the features provided by wordnet. It is simply a collection of synonyms. Consider the example given below:

from nltk.corpus import wordnet

syn = wordnet.synsets("cat")

print(syn**)**

The code gives the following result upon execution:

In the above example, we have invoked the synsets() *function to give us the synonyms for the word cat. We have assigned the output to the variable named* syn. *We have then printed out the values of this variable on the console.*

Wordnet also has a feature known as lexical relations which is a set of reciprocated semantic relations. Let us create a program that helps us to find the synonym and antonym of a certain word:

from nltk.corpus import wordnet

synonyms = []

```
antonyms = []

for s in wordnet.synsets("passive"):

    for lemm in s.lemmas():

        synonyms.append(lemm.name())

        if lemm.antonyms():

            antonyms.append(lemm.antonyms()[0].name())

        print(set(synonyms))

        print(set(antonyms))
```

In the above example, we are looking for *antonyms* and *synonyms* for the word *passive*.

We began by importing *wordnet* from *nltk.corpus*. We have then taken the list of antonyms and synonyms as empty and we will use these for appending purposes.

We have then passed the word *passive* to find its synonyms from the synsets module then we append them to the list synonyms and repeated it for the second one.

Finally, we have printed the output.

The code gives the result given below upon execution:

Fixing Word Lengthening

Word lengthening refers to the process of repeating characters. In English, words can only have a maximum of two characters repeated. Any additional characters should be done away with; otherwise, we may be dealing with misleading information. We can use the regular expressions' library to help us remove any repeated characters from our text. Let us create a function for doing that:

```
import re

def remove_lengthening(text):

    patt = re.compile(r"(.)\1{2,}")

    return patt.sub(r"\1\1", text)

print(remove_lengthening( "commmmmmmitttteeee" ))
```

The code will return the result given below when executed:

We have created a function named *remove_lengthening* which takes our text as the input. We have then created a variable named *patt* which helps us define the pattern that characters in our words should take. We had three characters which had been lengthened, that is, *m, t* and *e*. The function has reduced them to two which is a perfect match. However, consider the following example:

```
import re

def remove_lengthening(text):

    patt = re.compile(r"(.)\1{2,}")

    return patt.sub(r"\1\1", text)

print(remove_lengthening( "accccctive" ))
```

The code gives the following example upon execution:

The character c was lengthened. However, it was reduced to a length of 2. The word is spelled as *"active"* rather than *"active"*. This shows why we need to do spelling correction even after reducing the lengthening.

Spell Correction

This is the process by which the spelling of a word is corrected. Spell correction algorithms work based on min-edit functions since brute forcing one's may take too much time.

For the mid-edit functions to work effectively, word lengthening should be used first. This means that our spell correction will depend on the word lengthening. NLTK comes with no spell correction module, but there are numerous other libraries that we can use to perform this task. We will be using pattern en for this task.

To install the library, run the following command:

pip3 install pattern

You can then write the following code to demonstrate how length removal and soell correction can be done in *NLP*:

import re

from pattern.en import spelling

def remove_lengthening(text):

  patt = re.compile(r"(.)\1{2,}")

  return patt.sub(r"\1\1", text)

word = "accccctiiiive"

word_wlf = remove_lengthening(word) #calling the above function

print(*word_wlf*) #word lengthening cannot fix it completely

final_word = spelling(word_wlf)

print(final_word)

We began by removing the lengthening. This was done by defining a function named *remove_lengthening*. It is in this method that we have defined that a word should not have a character that exceeds a length of 2. When we passed the word accccctiiiive to the function, it returned *acctiive*. However, the word is still not correct. We need to perform spell correction on the word. That is why we have invoked the *spelling() function* which we imported from *pattern.en* and passed the result of lengthening removal to it. This should return the correct spelling of the word which is *active*.

Chapter 14: Using Jupyter notebook for user interaction

Display tabular data in IPython notebook

While working in an IPython notebook, in addition to plain text your program can produce output in HTML format. This code snippet shows how to format food data as an HTML table and display it in an IPython workbook.HTML class needs to be imported from IPython.display module. Because the code for making the table might be reused, we will put it in a separate function that accepts two arguments:

- *header - list of strings that are column headers*
- *data - list of lists representing rows*

Row elements might be either strings or numbers - we will convert them to strings on the fly.

```
from IPython.display import HTML

def make_table(header,data):

    # Constructing a HTML table

    html_string='<table border="1">'

    html_string+='<tr style="background: #ccc;"><th>'

    html_string+='</th><th style="width: 7em; text-align:
right;">'.join(header)+"</th></tr>" # make header row
```

```
for food in data:

    food_list=[str(a) for a in food]

    html_string+="<tr><td>"+'</td><td style="width: 7em;
text-align: right;">'.join(food_list)+"</td></tr>" # make data
row

    html_string+="</table>"

    RETURN HTML(html_string) # Create a html object from a
string

t=make_table(header,data)  # Create table from header and
data

t                    # show in in IPython workbook
```

Generated table is shown in the notebook

food	carb	fat	protein	calories	serving size
chicken breast	0.0	3.0	22.0	120.0	112.0
parmesan grated	0.0	1.5	2.0	20.0	5.0
pasta	39.0	1.0	7.0	210.0	56.0
potato	28.0	0.0	3.0	110.0	148.0
sour cream	1.0	5.0	1.0	60.0	30.0

Adding user interaction

While exploring data, it is often useful to play with several parameters interactively to find optimal values. IPython notebook allows such interactivity with a simple user interface you can embed in notebooks. This user interface is relatively limited - you can not create complex widget layouts and some user interface functions, such as selecting and opening a file, are not available for security reasons. We will explore creating real graphical user interface (GUI) programs later. Now, let's add some interactive tools to our notebook.

We will create an IPython notebook that calculates the nutrient and energy content of a dish using our ingredient table. The dish will contain chicken breast, pasta, and parmesan. The user will adjust the amount of each ingredient in grams using sliders. Notebook will calculate the amounts of major nutrients and the energy value of entire dish - showing this information in a table and displaying a pie chart that shows the relative amount of major nutrients.

For this we will need to import some facilities from the library:

- *HTML to show an HTML formatted table*
- *interact to create sliders that allow the user to adjust the amounts of ingredients and*
- *pyplot that allows to create graphs*

We will also use IPython's 'magic' command that tells it to embed graphs in a notebook

%matplotlib inline

Without this command, plots will appear in a separate window. The program header will look like this

from IPython.display import HTML

from ipywidgets import interact

import matplotlib.pyplot as plt

%matplotlib inline

To easily look up ingredient information given ingredient's name we will store this data not in a list as we did before but in a dictionary. Unlike lists dictionaries are unordered containers of key:value pairs. Python's strings can serve as keys; so, we will use the ingredient names as keys and their data as values. The part of the program dealing with reading food data from the file will change slightly:

```
data={}  # create an empty list to hold data

with open('ingredients.txt', 'rt') as f:
    for i,line in enumerate(f):
        fields=line.strip().split('\t')
        if i==0:
            header=fields  # remember a header
            continue
        food=fields[0].lower()
```

```
try:

    numbers=[float(n) for n in fields[1:]]

except:

    print(i,line)

    print(i,fields)

    continue

numbers=[float(n) for n in fields[1:]]

data[food]=numbers # append food info to data list
```

```
print(data)
```

Now, the food name becomes a key in the dictionary. It must be unique. If we have two foods with identical names in our file, information will be overwritten. The values stored are a list of the carbs, fat, energy value, and protein per serving, and serving size.

Every time the user adjusts the amount of an ingredient, we will need to calculate the amounts of carbs, fat, and protein supplied by each component and calculate the total amounts of carb, fat, protein, and calories in a dish.

Lets write a function that will take the food name and the quantity of it in a dish and calculate how many carbs, fats, proteins, and calories this ingredient contributes to the dish:

```
def get_share(food, quantity):

    serving=data[food][4]
```

```
nutrients=[round(a*quantity/serving,2)

        for a in data[food][:4]]

return nutrients
```

First, we look up the serving size for a given ingredient that is stored as the last element of the food description. Then, we use list comprehension on the per serving values of the carbs, fats, proteins, and calories stored in positions 0 through 3 by dividing the per serving values by serving size, multiplying them by the amount of the ingredient in a dish, rounding to two decimal positions, and returning the result.

Next, we need to create a function that will be called every time user adjusts the amount of an ingredient. This function will use all the values user can adjust using interactive widgets as parameters. The default values of the parameters allow IPython to guess what values are expected and what widgets to use for the interface. We want to adjust the amounts of ingredients in grams, that should be floating point numbers between 0 and 100. The names of the parameters will be used as labels for the widgets. So, the function will look like this:

```
def show_results(chicken=(0.0,100.0),

        pasta=(0.0,100.0),

        parmesan=(0.0,100.0)):

dish_content=[['<b>Total:</>',0,0,0,0]]

dish_content.append(['chicken']+
```

```
        get_share('chicken breast', chicken))
    dish_content.append(['pasta']+
        get_share('pasta', pasta))
    dish_content.append(['parmesan']+
        get_share('parmesan grated', parmesan))
    FOR column IN range(1,5): #Get sum for each column
        column_sum=sum([a[column]
                for a in dish_content[1:]])
        dish_content[0][column]=round(column_sum,2)
    # draw a pie plot
    plt.pie(dish_content[0][1:4],
        autopct='%1.1f%%',
        labels=('carbs','fat','protein'),
        colors=('palegreen','gold','salmon'))
    plt.show()
    return make_table(header[:-1],dish_content)
```

The function itself must draw a table. For a header, we can use the header we have read from a file, discarding the last element "serving size".

Variabledish_content will contain table data as a list of rows.

Rows are lists containing the ingredient name in the first element followed by the contribution of the given ingredient to the total number of carbs, fats, proteins, and calories in the dish.

The first row shows the total content in a dish. So, we create a row["Total:",0,0,0,0] and calculate the total carbs, fats, proteins, and calories later when the contributions of all the ingredients are known.

The contribution of each component is calculated by a functionget_share.

Finally, we go through the columns of the created table and fill the Totalvalues in the first row by summing up the values of each column. List comprehension ondish_contentis used to get a list of values in each column, and a standard librarysum() function is used to sum them up. The column sums are stored in the first row of the table.

The total values of the 3 major nutrients are then used to create a pie chart for the dish content. The functionpie from module matplotlibtakes the amount of carbs, fats, and proteins, and draws a pie chart using them. Parameters, labels, and colors are self-explanatory and define the labels and colors of the sectors, while the parameterautopctdefines a formatting string for the percentage of each ingredient in a dish. It means that the percentage should be printed as a floating point number with at least one digit before the decimal point and one after the decimal point, followed by '%'.plt.show() to show the chart in the notebook.

Finally, the functionshow_resultscalls amake_table with a header and a list of rows and returns the HTML element, which ensures the table will be shown in the notebook.

To create a user interface and an event loop that will automatically call theshow_resultsfunction, we use the functioninteractimported fromipywidgets by giving it the name of the function to call when user changes any controls:

interact(show_results)

Here is the entire listing:

from IPython.display import HTML

from ipywidgets import interact

import matplotlib.pyplot as plt

%matplotlib inline

data={} # create an empty list to hold data

with *open*('ingredients.txt', 'rt') as f:

    for i,line in *enumerate*(f):

        fields=line.strip().split('\t')

        if i==0:

            header=fields # *remember a header*

            continue

        food=fields[0].lower()

        try:

```python
        numbers=[float(n) for n in fields[1:]]
    except:
        print(i,line)
        print(i,fields)
        continue
    numbers=[float(n) for n in fields[1:]]
    data[food]=numbers # append food info to data list
print(data)
def make_table(header,data):
    # Constructing a HTML table
    html_string='<table border="1">'
    html_string+='<tr style="background: #ccc;"><th>'
    # make header row
    html_string+='''</th><th style="width: 7em;
        text-align:right;">'''.join(header)+"</th></tr>"
    for food in data:
        food_list=[str(a) for a in food]
        # make data row
        html_string+="<tr><td>"
        html_string+='''</td><td style="width: 7em;
```

```python
            text-align:right;">'".join(food_list)
        html_string+="</td></tr>"
    html_string+="</table>"
    # Create a html object from a string

    return HTML(html_string)
def get_share(food, quantity):
    serving=data[food][4]
    nutrients=[round(a*quantity/serving,2)
            for a in data[food][:4]]
    return nutrients
def show_results(chicken=(0.0,100.0),
            pasta=(0.0,100.0),
            parmesan=(0.0,100.0)):
    dish_content=[['<b>Total:</>',0,0,0,0]]
    dish_content.append(['chicken']+
            get_share('chicken breast', chicken))
    dish_content.append(['pasta']+
            get_share('pasta', pasta))
    dish_content.append(['parmesan']+
            get_share('parmesan grated', parmesan))
    for column in range(1,5):
```

```python
    column_sum=sum([a[column]

            for a in dish_content[1:]])

    dish_content[0][column]=round(column_sum,2)

    plt.pie(dish_content[0][1:4],

        autopct='%1.1f%%',

        labels=('carbs','fat','protein'),

        colors=('palegreen','gold','salmon'))

    plt.show()

    return make_table(header[:-1],dish_content)

interact(show_results)
```

If you find calculations to be time consuming, you might consider another function -interact_manual. It adds a button to the interface and its target function will only be called when the button is pressed. So you can adjust several controls without waiting for unnecessary calculations to complete.

Interact also offers other kinds of widgets: check box, text entry box, drop down list. The widget kind is guessed from the default arguments of a target function. The following snippet will create an interface that consists of a check box, text entry box, drop down list and a Run button you need to push to call the target function that prints the parameters it receives.

```python
from ipywidgets import interact_manual

def target( a=True,
```

```
        b='abc',

        c=['one', 'two', 'three'],

        d={'apple':1, 'pear':2, 'orange':3}):

    print(a,b,c,d)

    return

i=interact_manual(target)
```

Alternatively, an interactive function might be used to create a control box that serves as a parent of multiple widgets. These widgets might be constructed by explicit constructor calls, which gives the user more control. In addition, the state of those controls might be altered from within a program. See IPython documentation for more information on available controls.

Chapter 15: The Regular Expressions

We need to take a little detour here and explore a bit what we are able to do with the regular expressions when working in the Python language. One of the things that you are going to enjoy when it comes to the larger library that is in Python is that you can work with something that is known as a regular expression, or an expression that is responsible for handling any kind of task that you would like without all of the glitches, and that are able to handle all of the different searches that you want to do with these.

You will find that working on these regular expressions are going to be good to use in Python because it helps us to go through a large variety of text, including text strings if you would like, and it is possible to use these types of regular expressions to check out the string or the text in your code to double-check whether everything is going to match up in the code in the proper manner or not.

These regular expressions can actually be nice to work with and when you would like to work on one, you can need to stick with the same kind of expression through it, even if you are going to work with another kind of coding language along with Python. Let's say that you are doing some work and you want to code with not only Python but also with other languages like C++ or Java. You would still be able to work with the regular expressions and stick with the syntax that you are familiar with when working on Python.

At this point, we have talked a bit about the regular expressions, but we need to dive in a bit deeper and get more information about it. One of the methods that you can use when it is time to explore these regular expressions is to do a search through the code for a word that you may have spelled out in different ways for your text editor. Maybe you went through and typed out blue in one part, and bleu in another part and you want to get it fixed out, the regular expressions are going to make it easier for you to see it happen.

Any time that you would like to work with some of these regular expressions, it is important to start out by going to the library with Python and then importing the expressions that they have there. You need to do this right now before we start to go much further, or it can be a challenge to do the work later on. Think about all of the different kinds of libraries and extensions that you will need at the beginning of any project and then add these in as well.

There are going to be a few different types of regular expressions that you are going to be able to use when you try to write out some of your own codes. Often, these are going to show up along with the statements, and you must be able to work with them to get the expressions to work the way that you want. To make sure that they work though, we need to spend some time looking at the background and the basics that are going to show up. So, let's get started with learning more about how these regular expressions work.

Basic Patterns

One of the things that a programmer is going to notice when they start with the expressions is that these don't just specify out the character that is fixed that you want to use in the code. In fact, it is possible to bring them out in some cases and use them to find all of the patterns that are going to show up in your code. Some of the different patterns that you need to show up in your statement, as well as in some of the other parts of a Python code, will include:

1. Ordinary characters. These are characters that will match themselves exactly. Be careful with using some of these because they do have special meanings inside of Python. The characters that you will need to watch out for include [], *, ^, $

2. The period—This is going to match any single except the new line symbol of '\n'

3. \w—This is the lowercase w that is going to match the "word" character. This can be a letter, a digit, or an underbar. Keep in mind that this is the

mnemonic and that it is going to match a single word character rather than the whole word.

4. \b—This is the boundary between a non-word and a word.

5. \s—This is going to match a single white space character including the form, form, tab, return, newline, and even space. If you do \S, you are talking about any character that is not a white space.

6. ^ = start, $ = end—These are going to match to the end or the start of your string.

7. \t, \n, \r—These are going to stand for tab, newline, and return.

8. \d—This is the decimal digit for all numbers between 0 and 9. Some of the older regex utilities will not support this so be careful when using it.

9. \ --This is going to inhibit how special the character is. You use this if you are uncertain about whether the character has some special meaning or not to ensure that it is treated just like another character.

One of the ways that you are going to be able to use these regular expressions is to help you complete a query that you would like. There are other tasks, but we are going to focus on the idea of using a query to get things done. The three methods of doing a query with a regular expression that we are going to focus on are the re.findall(), re.search(), and re.match() functions. Let's take a look at what these can do and when we would be able to use these in our code.

First on the list is going to be the search method. To work with this, the syntax is going to include the function of search(). This is the one where you are able to match up things that show up at any location of the string. There aren't going to be some restrictions that you have to worry about when we work on this one, which makes it easier.

With the search method, you get the ability to check whether or not there is some kind of match that is found in the string. Sometimes, there will be a match and sometimes, there won't be based on the query that you make and what is in the code. If there are no matches in that string, then you won't get a result out of this. But if you do the query and the program comes up with a match within the string, no matter where it is found, then the result will be given back. With this one, it is only going to return the information once. There could be ten times the item is listed out, but this one will just show you that it is there, and how many times it is there. The code syntax that you are able to use with this one includes:

```
import re

string = 'apple, orange, mango, orange'

match = re.search(r'orange', string)

print(match.group(0))
```

The second thing that you can do with this is the match method. You can use this option in the same kind of code that we had before, but it is going to go through and look to see if the first word in the sequence is going to match up with your search. If the term is the first word in the sequence, then it is going to show up. If it is not, then you won't be able to get the term that you would like.

In the example above, we would be looking for the orange and seeing if we could find a match that goes with it. But since orange is not listed out as the first word in that sequence, we would not be able to get a match, even though the word orange is present. For this one to work, we need to have it match up right in the first term that is there.

The third thing that we can work with here is the findall method. If you would like to do some work and look at a string, and then get a statement to show up to release all of the possibilities for one word out of the string, then this is the type of method that you would need to use. So, if you would like to use the code above and then figure out how many times the word orange shows up, you would want to work with the findall method instead.

So to keep this one simple and to allow it to work the right way, you would just need to use the syntax that we talked about above and switch out the part with the re.search() over to re.findall(). Then you would get a new result. For this one, since we are looking at orange, we would be able to get the result of "orange, orange" in the end. This is because this method is going to be used to tell us if there are patterns or how many times that a specific word or phrase is going to show up in the code. If you had put the word in five times in the code above, then the findall method would be able to list out the word orange five times as a result.

As you can see, all three of these regular expressions are going to work in a manner that is different in order to help you work on the codes that you want to write. Each of these methods will work in order to help you find the information that you need, look to see whether there is a pattern found in the information, and can help out with so much more. Take some time practicing these to see how they are able to help you get more done in your coding.

Chapter 16: Data Visualization with Python

Data visualization can be described as the various ways by which analyzed data i.e. information is displayed. Sometimes, even well-analyzed data is not informative enough at a glance. With data visualization, which includes line graphs, bar charts, pictograms, etc. the results/ analysis being presented become less abstract to the end-user, and decision-making is enhanced. In this chapter, we will be learning various techniques for displaying the results of our analysis with NumPy and Pandas frameworks.

Matplotlib

This is a python library for producing high-quality 2D plots. For those that have some MATLAB experience, the plotting techniques and visualizations here will seem familiar. Matplotlib offers a lot of flexibility with plots, in terms of control over things like the axes, fonts, line styles and size, etc. However, all these require writing extra lines of code. So, if you do not mind going the extra mile (with typing code) to fully specify your plots, then matplotlib is your friend. For extra information about this package, visit the official page at www.matplotlib.org

There are basically two approaches to plotting data in matplotlib: The Functional and the object-oriented (OO) approach, respectively. You might encounter the two terms consistently as you interact with programmers and other programming languages, but they are just two slightly different approaches to programming. We will only be considering the functional approach here, as it is easy to understand for beginners and also requires writing fewer lines of code. The OO method, however, offers more control over the plots at the consequence of writing more lines of code.

To start off, let us create a simple cosine plot using the functional approach.

First, let us import the relevant libraries and create plot data:

```
In []: import matplotlib.pyplot as plt
       import numpy as np
       %matplotlib inline
       # creating plot values
       x = np.linspace(0,10)  # x-axis/time-scale
       y = np.cos(x)   # corresponding cosine values
```

The %matplotlib inline option in the code ensures all our plots are displayed as we run each cell. If you are running a different python console, you can put plt.show() at the end of your code to display your plots. plt.show() is the print() function equivalent for matplotlib plots.

Functional method

```
In []: # functional plot
       plt.plot(x,y)
Out[]: [<matplotlib.lines.Line2D at 0x25108cf27f0>]
```

Notice that we get an Out[] statement. This is because we did not print the result using plt.show(). While this is not significant if you are using Jupyter, it might be required for other consoles.

We can also plot multiple functions in one graph.

In []: z = np.sin(x) # Adding an extra plot variable
plt.plot(x,y,x,z);plt.show()

To print multiple graphs, just pass each argument to the plot statement, and separate the plots with commas.

To make our graphs more meaningful, we can label the axes and give the graph a title.

In []: plt.plot(x,y,x,z)
plt.xlabel('Time axis') # *labelling x-axis*
plt.ylabel('Magnitude') # *labelling y-axis*
plt.title('Sine and Cosine waves') # *graph title*
plt.show() # *printing*
Output:

Now, this is a better figure. Since we added more than one plot, there is an extra functionality called 'legend' which helps differentiate between the plots.

The legend function takes in two arguments. The first is usually a string argument for labeling the graphs in order. The second is for extra functionality, like where the legend should be. The location argument is specified using 'loc=value'. For value = 1, upper right corner; 2, for upper left corner; 3, for lower left corner; and 4 for the lower right corner. However, if you would rather let matplotlib decide the best location, use 'value=0'.

In []: plt.plot(x,y,x,z)
plt.xlabel('Time axis')
plt.ylabel('Magnitude')
plt.title('Sine and Cosine waves')
plt.legend(['y','z'],loc=0)   # *loc=0 means best location*

plt.show()
Output:

Assuming we wish to plot both the cosine and sine wave above, but side by side.

We can use the subplot command to do this. Think of the subplot as an array of figures with a specification of the number of rows and columns. So, if we want just two graphs beside each otherhat can be considered as a 1 row, and 2 columns array.

In []:# subplotting
plt.subplot(1,2,1)   # *plot 1*
plt.plot(x,y)
plt.title('Cosine plot')
plt.subplot(1,2,2)   # *plot 2*
plt.plot(x,z)
plt.title('Sine plot')
plt.tight_layout()   # avoid overallping plots
plt.show()

Tip: The tight_layout() line ensures that all subplots are well spaced. Always use this when sub-plotting to make your plots nicer. Try removing that line and compare the output!

Output:

To explain the subplot line i.e. subplot(1,2,1) and subplot(1,2,2): The first two values are the number of rows and columns of the subplot. As seen in the above result, the plot is on one row, and two columns. The last value specifies the order of the plot; hence (1,2,1) translates to plotting that figure in the first row, and the first column out of two.

We can specify the line colors in our plots, as well as the line style. This is passed as a string after the plot argument. Since all the plot options, including marker style and the likes are exactly same as for Matlab, here is a link to Matlab plot documentation to explore all the extra customization feature you can port to your matplotlib   plots: https://www.mathworks.com/help/matlab/ref/plot.html#btzp ndl-1

Let us change the color and fonts in our subplots to illustrate this.

```
In []: plt.subplot(1,2,1)   # plot 1
plt.plot(x,y,'r-x')  # red plot with -x marker
plt.title('Cosine plot')
plt.subplot(1,2,2)   # plot 2
plt.plot(x,z,'g-o')  # green plot with -o marker
plt.title('Sine plot')
```

```
plt.tight_layout()    # still avoiding overallping plots
plt.show()
```
Output:

Exercise: Now that you have learned how to plot using the functional approach, test your skills.

Plot this:

Tip: *use np.arange(0,10,11) for the x-axis.*

After creating your plot, you may need to import it into your documents or just save it on your device. To do this, you can right-click the image in your Jupyter notebook and click copy. Then, you can paste the copied image into your document.

If you prefer to save, you can use the plt.savefig('figurename.extension', DPI = value) method. Here, figurename is the desired name for your saved image; The extension is the desired format i.e. PNG, JPG, BMP, etc. Finally, the DPI specifies the quality of the image, the higher the better. Usually for standard printing quality, about 300 is good enough.

Tip: Learning a bit more about these specifications can really help you generate better images from your plots.

Seaborn

This is another data visualization library that extends the graphical range of the matplotlib library. A lot of methods from matplotlib are applicable here, for customizing plots. However, it generates high quality, dynamic plots in fewer lines of code.

Seaborn is more optimized for plotting trends in datasets, and we are going to explore a dataset using this library. Since, Seaborn is pre-loaded with a few datasets (it can call and load certain datasets from its online repository), we will just load up one of these for our example.

Example 77: Loading a seaborn dataset and plotting trends

As with other packages, we have to import seaborn using the standard variable name 'sns'.

In []: # importing seaborn
import seaborn as sns
%matplotlib inline

Next, we will load the popular 'tips' dataset from Seaborn. This dataset contains information about a restaurant, the tips given to the waiters, amount of tip, size of the customer group (e.g. a party of 3 people) etc.

In []:# loading a dataset from seaborn
tips_dataset = sns.load_dataset('tips')
tips_dataset.head()
Out[]:

	total_bill	tip	sex	smoker	day	time	size
0	16.99	1.01	Female	No	Sun	Dinner	2

					Su	Dinn	
1	10.34	1.66	Male	No	n	er	3
2	21.01	3.50	Male	No	Su n	Dinn er	3
3	23.68	3.31	Male	No	Su n	Dinn er	2
4	24.59	3.61	Femal e	No	Su n	Dinn er	4

Next, we can find trends in the data using different kinds of plots. Let us use the dist_plot (distribution plot) to observe how the total_bill is distributed across the dataset.

In []:#Use distplot
sns.distplot(tips_dataset['total_bill'],bins = 30,kde=False)
Out[]:<matplotlib.axes._subplots.AxesSubplot at
        0x28d3867d6d8>

The distplot shows the distribution of certain trends within data. According to the plot above, we can infer that most of the bills are within the range of $10 - $20, since they have the tallest bins within the distribution. You may notice some extra arguments in the distplot code, the bins argument controls the number of histograms that are shown within the population. The higher the value, the more histograms. Although, sometimes higher can make the data less obvious to read, so finding a balance is important. The next argument is the 'kde', which means kernel density estimate. It is sometimes preferred over histograms, or along with histograms for a more accurate interpretation of the data. It is mostly an estimate of the probability density function of any variable within the distribution, more like the histogram but smoother. You can read up for a more thorough statistical background on some of these things.

Another useful plot is the relplot, which shows the relationship between two variables within a data_set. It is good for comparison, and can sort results based off categories i.e. sex, age, etc. within the data.

Let us demonstrate how the total_bill relates with the estimated tip, and sort by category male/female.

In []: # estimating tip with respect to total_bill
sns.relplot(x ="total_bill", y="tip", data = tips_dataset)
out []:
Here is a basic plot without the category argument. This tells us that the tips generally increase with respect to the total bill. The higher bills correspond to higher tips, and lower bills to lower tips. Adding categories makes the data more interesting as we can see the category that tips more or less.

In []: sns.relplot(x ="total_bill", y="tip", data = tips_dataset, hue = 'sex')
Out[]: <seaborn.axisgrid.FacetGrid at 0x28d3b9cedd8>
See how this is a more informative data. This tells how male customers tipped higher per total_bill on average than the females.

Now this idea can be extended and applied to more advanced data. You can further explore various plotting options with relplot via this link: www.seaborn.pydata.org/tutorial/relational.html

The relplot is even extended with the pairplot option, which relates everything in a data set in one plot. It is a great way to get a quick overview of important trends within your data.

In []: sns.pairplot(tips_dataset,hue = 'sex', palette = 'coolwarm')

Out[]:<seaborn.axisgrid.PairGrid at 0x28d412f2e48>

See how easy it is to observe the variations between the three main parameters within the data: total_bill, tip and size. The category 'sex' has also been passed to observe the trends in that wise. For each instance where a variable is being compared with itself, we get a kernel density estimate, or a histogram if specified. The other comparisons are made via scatterplots.

From the pairplot, we can quickly infer that the tips do not necessarily increase with increasing party size, considering that the largest tip is within the party size of 3. This inference can be found by observing graphs 2,3, and 3,2 (row,column).

You may wonder, could we also find the population size within a dataset by category? Well, countplot is very useful for that. It is common to see such kinds of plots within a document like the US census report. It basically displays a bar chart, with the height corresponding to the population of a category within the dataset.

In []:sns.countplot(x ='sex', data = tips_dataset)

Out[]: <matplotlib.axes._subplots.AxesSubplot at
0x28d41990978>

To validate this, we can use the pandas groupby method along with count. Hope you can recall these methods!

In []: import pandas as pd   #importing pandas to use
groupby()

tips_dataset.groupby('sex').count()

Out[]:

sex	total_bill	tip	smoker	day	time	size
Male	157	157	157	157	157	157
Female	87	87	87	87	87	87

As expected, notice how the male and female counts of 157 and 87 respectively correspond with the countplot above.

These and many more are data visualization capabilities of Seaborn. For now, these are some basic examples to get you started; you may visit the seaborn official documentation gallery to explore more plots styles and options via this link: https://seaborn.pydata.org/examples/index.html

Pandas

Well, it's our friendly pandas again. The library also has some highly functional visualization capabilities. It is quite intuitive at the time to use these built-in visualization options while working with pandas, unless something more specialized is required.

First, we import a few familiar libraries:

```
In []: # importing all necessary libraries
import numpy as np
import pandas as pd
import matplotlib.pyplot as plt
%matplotlib inline
import seaborn as sns
```

You may wonder why all the other libraries apart from Pandas are imported. Well, your outputs will look much better with these libraries synchronized. Pandas plots using the matplotlib library functionality -- even though it doesn't directly call it, and the seaborn library makes the graphs/plots look better.

Let us work with a different dataset. We can create our own data frame and call plots off it.

We will create a data frame from a uniform distribution.

```
In []: # let us create our dictionary
d = {'A':np.random.rand(5),
      'B':np.random.rand(5),
      'C':np.random.rand(5),
      'D':np.random.rand(5)}
```

```
# now creating a data frame
df = pd.DataFrame(d)
df
```

Out[]:

	A	B	C	D
0	0.982520	0.469717	0.973735	0.397019
1	0.602272	0.148608	0.433559	0.929647
2	0.566168	0.737165	0.040840	0.435978
3	0.632309	0.772419	0.341389	0.603980
4	0.949631	0.906318	0.895018	0.679825

With our data frame, we can now observe trends. To create a histogram plot using pandas, use the hist() function. Also, you can pass some matplotlib arguments like 'bins'

```
In []: df[['A']].hist(bins=30)
Out[]: array([[<matplotlib.axes._subplots.AxesSubplot object at
        0x0000028D432E50B8>]],
    dtype=object)
```

We can do an area plot of the values as well, which is essentially a line graph of the values with the area underneath shaded:

```
In []: df.plot.area()
Out[]: <matplotlib.axes._subplots.AxesSubplot at
        0x28d433b2438>
```

The transparency settings of this graph can be set with the argument 'alpha = value'.

We can also do a bar plot which can categorize our data based off of our row_index.

In []: df.plot.bar()
Out[]: <matplotlib.axes._subplots.AxesSubplot at
     0x28d435fe828>

See, our x-axis has the row index, and the y-axis shows the value of in each column per index.

This kind of plot can be useful for things like, sales trends per month (with sales as values and months as row_index), school attendance per day, etc. Our current plots might not be too informative since we are using random data, however, an actual data set would reveal more details.

If you prefer, the bar plots can be stacked to give better visualization:

In []: df.plot.bar(stacked = True, alpha = 0.8)
Out[]: <matplotlib.axes._subplots.AxesSubplot at
     0x28d43a6e048>

This kind of plot gives us an idea of the total values per category, as well as the percentages that account for that total. We can still observe that value in column 'A' contributes the most in category '0', followed by 'C', and so forth.

Line plot:

In []: df.plot.line(y =['B','C'])

Out[]: <matplotlib.axes._subplots.AxesSubplot at
    0x28d43b6fc88>

The line plot takes positional arguments of the x and y-axis. In this case, the y-axis has been specified. Other specifications like: line width 'lw', figsize, etc. can be included as well.

We can also make a scatterplot, box plots and a few other plots that can be useful for interpreting data. Depending on your choice, and proficiency with these plotting techniques, you will be able to master data and the information it contains.

Go ahead and check these useful links for extra information on plotting with pandas:

https://towardsdatascience.com/introduction-to-data-
    visualization-in-python-89a54c97fbed
https://pandas.pydata.org/pandas-
    docs/stable/user_guide/visualization.html

With these data visualization options, you may start to test your skills by displaying data in a whole range of formats. It is quite obvious that a good knowledge of statistical methods would be very useful for excelling as a data scientist, since data science mostly deals with statistical data. While statistics can be intimidating without graphical aides, your own approach will be better as you now have the full potential of matplotlib, seaborn and pandas to visualize your lessons. For interactive visualization options (not covered here), you can check out 'plotly and cufflinks' libraries from this link: https://plot.ly/ipython-notebooks/cufflinks/

Conclusion

Thank you for making it through to the end. This book presented an overview of Python programming and utilities of using Python to develop applications. The book also presented the basic programming syntax of Python for absolute beginners with no background in programming. We presented the functionalities of the NumPy, Pandas and matplotlib libraries. These libraries provide efficient tools to handle, process and visualize large datasets.

After finishing this book, you would develop skills in developing modules and functions in Python, loading and importing modules in Python. You would also develop skills in loading and exporting dataset from and to Python environments. You would also acquire skills in analysis and processing datasets using both libraries NumPy and Pandas by handling missing data and exploring datasets. You would develop skill in visualizing data using different type of graphs as well by mastering the functionalities of the matplotlib library.

Overall this book provides a guide on to use these handy libraries in data analysis. Once you have acquired these skills and know the functionalities of the NumPy, Pandas and Matplotlib libraries, you will be able to analyze any data you have in hand using Python. You also develop more advanced skills to handle complex datasets.